HD
6073
.T42   Farm to factory
U53

Farm to Factory

Saturday, March 8th, 1834

View of Lowell, Massachusetts.

FARM to FACTORY

Women's Letters, 1830-1860

Edited by Thomas Dublin

DISCARDED

 Columbia University Press • New York • 1981

Library of Congress Cataloging in Publication Data
Main entry under title:

Farm to factory.

Includes bibliographical references.
1. Women—Employment—New England—History.
2. Women—New England—Correspondence. 3. Textile
workers—New England—Correspondence. I. Dublin,
Thomas, 1946–
HD6073.T42U53   331.4'877'00974   80-28084
ISBN 0-231-05118-2   AACR1

Columbia University Press
New York   Guildford, Surrey

Contents

Illustrations

Acknowledgments

I began work on this book six years ago, quite unknowingly at the time. As I completed work on my doctoral dissertation, I grew increasingly dissatisfied with my almost complete reliance on quantitative data drawn from company payrolls and manuscript censuses. I began to search for letters, diaries, and reminiscences that would speak to the consciousness of women workers in the early textile mills of New England. From that search came the collections of letters that are brought together in this volume.

My first debts encountered in this process have been to archivists and individuals who have helped me find and understand the letters of mill women and to institutions that have granted me permission to reprint letters from their holdings. I am grateful to Barbara Brasseur who first loaned the Bennett Letters to the Merrimack Valley Textile Museum, where I had a chance to examine them initially, and to Betsy Tunis who first told me about the letters of Delia Page. I would also like to express my appreciation to the Vermont Historical Society, the New Hampshire Historical Society, the Massachusetts Historical Society, the Haverhill Public Library, and to Mildred Tunis for granting permission to reprint the edited letters here. For permission to quote brief portions of letters in the introductory essay, I would like to acknowledge Harry and Mary Dinmore, Aileen Eurich, and the Schlesinger Library, Radcliffe College.

The letters provide a starting point for this book, but illustrations add a life and concreteness of their own. For permission to use illustrations I would like to thank Baker Library, Harvard Business School, Colby-Sawyer College, Haverhill Public Library, Lowell Historical Society, Lowell Museum, Manchester Historic Association, Merrimack Valley Textile Museum, New Britain Museum of American Art, New Hampshire Historical Society, New York Historical Association, Old Sturbridge Village, Shelburne Museum, Mildred Tunis, and the University of Lowell.

Financial support has sped this work along at several crucial junctures.

A Regents' Faculty Fellowship from the University of California, San Diego, support from the Research Committee of the Academic Senate, and a grant-in-aid from the Merrimack Valley Textile Museum have provided me with the time and the resources I have needed to carry out this work. Numerous individuals helped in the process of transcribing and typing the letters; I particularly thank Lucy Duvall, Carmen Martinez, Colleen O'Connor, and Jean Proctor for their efforts.

Once I had typescripts of the letters, the work of tracing the writers and placing their experience in context began. I did almost all of this work while teaching in California, and could not possibly have carried it out without the assistance of Fran Rudman and Elaine Banks of the Interlibrary Loan Department at the University of California, San Diego. Other U.C.S.D. colleagues have provided helpful assistance. Ric Accurso and Michael O'Hagan greatly lightened my burden as I prepared a computer version of the letters, Larry Cruse shared his knowledge of maps, and Eunice Konold contributed her genealogical expertise several times during the course of my work. Numerous New Englanders helped me as well and answered what must at times have seemed like endless requests for additional information. In particular, I have benefited from the efforts of Florence Bartoshesky, Deborah Bruns, Michael Folsom, Lewis Karabatsos, Elizabeth Lessard, Martha Mayo, Betsy and Mildred Tunis, R. Stuart Wallace, and Helena Wright.

Since I first discussed this book with him several years ago, Bernard Gronert of Columbia University Press has been unfailing in his support and encouragement. I would also like to express special thanks to Jennifer Crewe, Lee Chong, and Gerard Mayers for their editorial, design, and production support. This is a better book for their efforts.

Portions of two of these collections of letters have appeared in print in somewhat different form, and permission to reprint that material is gratefully acknowledged. Several of the Hodgdon letters appeared in "The Hodgdon Family Letters: A View of Women in the Early Textile Mills, 1830-1840," *Historical New Hampshire* (1978), 33:283-95, and the first seven of Mary Paul's letters were published in "The Letters of Mary Paul, 1845-1849," *Vermont History* (1980), 48:77-88.

Finally, I have benefited from the criticism and suggestions of friends and colleagues who read the manuscript as it went through numerous drafts. Penny Dublin, Gary Kulik, Carol Lasser, Patricia Rosas, Mary Ryan, Betsy and Mildred Tunis, and Helena Wright have all made helpful contributions in this respect. What problems remain are largely a function of my own version of "Yankee independence," a stubbornness I share with several of the authors of the letters presented below.

Farm to Factory

Introduction

FEW PEOPLE have ever heard of Sarah Hodgdon, Louisa Sawyer, Persis Edwards, Mary Paul, or Delia Page. And, at first glance, there seems no reason why anyone should have. These women were not famous or influential in their own time. They probably did not even stand out in the towns and neighborhoods in which they lived. They have three things in common, however, that rescue them from total obscurity and make them of interest today: they all worked in New England textile factories before the Civil War, they wrote or received letters while working in these mills, and finally, their letters have survived to the present, offering rare glimpses into the everyday lives and experiences of rather ordinary American women.

Although all of these letters were written by women mill workers or members of their immediate families, we do well to view them within a broader compass. The women who wrote or received the letters did work in the mills, but they were not lifelong mill workers, born and raised under the shadow of the factory. They were daughters of self-respecting farmers, and mill employment was simply one of a number of options open to them. As the letters indicate, they shifted readily from one occupation to another. Ann Blake, for instance, worked in a Nashua, New Hampshire mill for a single summer before entering a dressmaking shop, where she remained for two years. After four years in the Lowell mills, Mary Paul set up shop in Brattleboro, Vermont making pants and coats. Soon tiring of that trade, she entered a utopian community for a year and then worked briefly as a housekeeper before marrying at the age of twenty-seven. Furthermore, the collections reprinted here include a number of letters written by members of mill workers' families. Olive Sawyer Brown, whose sister Louisa worked in Lowell for fourteen years, married at eighteen and described her life as a farmer's wife, "in the woods among the stumps and owls." Elizabeth Hodgdon wrote home describing her feelings as a teacher, holding sway as President of her "little repub-

lic," as she called her classroom. Sarah and Mary Trussell present views
of the school setting from the student's perspective in letters to their
foster sister, Delia Page, who was at work in the mills of the Amoskeag
Company in Manchester. The letter writers thus delineate the range of
girls' and women's activities in the antebellum period.

It is precisely because these women were not extraordinary that their
letters are so important. Increasingly, historians are becoming aware of
the need to expand our vision of history to incorporate the experiences of
the not-so-famous Americans who have until now found scant place in
the story of our nation's past. To limit history to the study of presidents,
generals, and leading reformers is to focus only on the most visible and
accessible individuals and events in the past. Such a view is not only
incomplete; it is, more importantly, distorted.

To clarify this point, consider how we would react today to a history of
slavery written entirely from the perspective of slaveowners, or a history
of American Indians based entirely on the testimony of military men and
politicians committed to the opening up of Indian lands to white settlement. Slaveowners, generals, and politicians were certainly more prolific
writers and have left a fuller trail of primary documents than have slaves
or Indians, but their testimony must of necessity reflect their place within
history. Especially where cultural conflicts and power differences are important elements in the historical process, we must try to find evidence of
the values, attitudes, and actions of all parties in the struggle.

In this light the family letters of women textile workers take on particular signficance. In the history of textile manufacturing, the writings of
millowners and agents have held a prominent place. These were the
men—and they were all men—who conceived the mill village and the
factory town and who directed the activities of workers within the factories that came to dot the New England landscape in the first half of the
nineteenth century. They created a paternalistic system that employed
and controlled young women drawn into the mills from the surrounding
countryside. Given their pre-eminent power they deserve a major place
in any discussion of the history of the industry. And historians have
certainly accorded them this place. Some historians have praised their
contributions; others would emphasize the enormous profits they enjoyed and point to their evident exploitation of female labor. A problem
with each of these perspectives is a tendency to focus entirely on the
millowners and agents, and thus treat the mill women as relatively inert
and passive elements in the historical process. One way to escape the
limitations of this view is to place the women themselves at center stage
and, through their letters, permit them to speak for themselves.

Although few women are represented in this volume, they were not isolated or atypical individuals. Between 1830 and 1860 tens of thousands of young, single women—much like these letter writers—left their hill-country farms in northern New England and sought employment in the expanding factory towns. They worked in the red brick mills of Lowell, Chicopee, Holyoke, and Lawrence in Massachusetts, of Manchester, Nashua, and Dover in New Hampshire, and of Saco and Biddeford in Maine, to name only the largest of the mill towns that emerged in these years. They worked in the factories for a few years and then returned to their native homes, moved west, or married and settled in the growing urban centers. For a brief period these farm women lived and worked in an urban, industrial milieu. Their letters permit us to reflect on the human significance of this experience.

I have brought together four sets of letters written by women mill workers or members of their immediate families in the years between 1830 and 1861. The collections represent only a small portion of extant letters but, by focusing on a limited number of individuals, we can trace their experiences in depth and over a period of years.[1] This introduction seeks to establish the larger context within which they wrote. Here I examine a number of themes that are common to the letters and that link the experience of mill women to broad trends in women's history in the middle decades of the nineteenth century. Then I discuss the economic and social forces that produced an urban migration of this magnitude, and go on to consider the kinds of women who migrated. Finally, I explore the place of the mill experience within the life cycle of rural women in these decades. With this basis established, we may then shift our focus and examine the letters themselves.

Many of the themes that emerge from the letters suggest aspects of nineteenth-century life that working women shared with all women, and that permeated the lives of men as well. Three seem worthy of mention. First, these writers express repeated concerns regarding sickness and death, reminding readers today how immediate and pressing these problems were in their daily lives. In the first collection of letters, John Hodgdon writes his millhand sister Sarah that a Mr. Hayes "Layes at the point of Deth," while in a subsequent letter Elizabeth Hodgdon describes the

1. The four sets of letters include: Hodgdon Family Letters, New Hampshire Historical Society, and Elizabeth Hodgdon Letters in Sanborn Family Papers, Massachusetts Historical Society (hereafter cited as MHS); Bennett Family Letters, Haverhill Public Library, Haverhill, Mass.; Mary Paul Letters, Vermont Historical Society; Delia Page Letters, Tracy Memorial Library, New London, N.H., courtesy of Mildred Tunis. In future notes I will only note locations of letters that are not reprinted below.

death at sea of their cousin, John Brewster. Olive Sawyer's first letter to Sabrina Bennett notes her brother Samuel's bout with fever and dysentery and two letters later she informs Sabrina of the death of another brother, Jeremiah, from typhoid fever. He died while working in Lowell, tended by his millhand sisters, Hepzibah and Louisa. These few examples are multiplied tenfold in the letters themselves. Luther Trussell may have summed things up most aptly in writing to his foster daughter, Delia Page: "Thare is no news. Nobody dead or married."[2]

Another element that may seem distant to contemporary readers is the centrality of religion and religious sensibilities in these women's lives.[3] Weathly Page, writing from her boardinghouse in Lowell, exhorted her friends back home: "When you feel to pour out your soul to God and direct your prayers to the throne of mercy then don't forget us who are distant from you." These lines had more than rhetorical meaning to Wealthy and her correspondents. Particularly in times of sickness religion proved an important source of solace. Olive Sawyer described the profound changes that her brother Samuel experienced as he struggled with fever: "He called me to his bed side and told me to seek religion. O Sabrina I wish you had been here so that we could have wept together. It was a time of rejoicing. He was one of the most happy creatures I ever saw." Samuel soon recovered, but his brother Jeremiah did not fare so well; on his deathbed, however, he took strength from his beliefs. Wrote Olive: "O said he that religion that was my comfort in health is my support now. He longed to go and be with his Saviour. About fifteen minutes before he died he sang two verses of Alas and did my Saviour bleed with a loud and clear voice."[4] The women letter writers placed great store in religion and they rejoiced especially when the men in their families expressed similar faith. Religion was much more important in the daily lives of women than of men, but in moments of crisis both acknowledged its centrality.

Finally, these letters reveal the importance of family and kinship bonds for women, even in the face of repeated migrations that often caused

2. John Hodgdon to Sarah Hodgdon, March 29, 1840; Elizabeth Hodgdon to Sarah Hodgdon, April 21, 1842, Sanborn Family Papers, MHS; Olive Sawyer to Sabrina Bennett, Sept. 25, 1836, Nov. 14, 1840; Luther M. Trussell to Delia Page, June 20, 1860, Delia Page Letters.

3. For a much fuller treatment of these themes, see Nancy F. Cott, *The Bonds of Womanhood: "Woman's Sphere" in New England, 1780-1835* (New Haven: Yale University Press, 1977), ch. 4.

4. Wealthy Page to "Respected Friends," June 6, 1830; Olive Sawyer to Sabrina Bennett, Sept. 25, 1837, Nov. 14, 1840, see below.

family separations. The Sabrina Bennett Letters are particularly remark-
able on this score. Sabrina Bennett lived with her parents in Haverhill,
Massachusetts in the 1830s and 1840s, during which period she kept up
an active correspondence with assorted cousins and aunts. She saved a
fair number of these letters, permitting us a glimpse into one such extended kinship network. Sabrina's mother was one of eleven Edwards
children who lived to marry, and among them these siblings had forty
children. Sabrina Bennett had ten aunts, ten uncles, and more than thirty
first cousins on her mother's side alone. Six cousins and two aunts are
included among the authors of surviving letters, but almost all of the
cousins are mentioned at some point in the letters.[5] Some married, a few
died, and others worked with letter writers or sent their best wishes to
Sabrina in another's letter. It is clear that these cousins, especially the
women among them, comprised a close-knit, though physically wide-
spread, kinship network. They were moving about New England—sometimes living at home, at other times working on their own, but always in
touch with one another and sharing the latest developments in their lives.
In their letters we see an element of family life that has disappeared in
the past 150 years. Families in the mid-nineteenth century were essen-
tially nuclear, consisting almost exclusively of married couples and their
unmarried children. Nevertheless, "family" had an extensive dimension
far exceeding the limits of the nuclear family and the letters offer evidence of affective bonds that radiated from the immediate family living
together. Declining fertility and long-distance migration have undermined wider kinship ties in recent years to the point that extended kinship networks in the United States today are a pale shadow of their
nineteenth-century counterparts.

The letter writers shared much in common with other rural women in
these decades, but by going to mill towns they experienced a new urban
setting in sharp contrast to the farming communities in which they grew
up. What sort of world did these women enter when they left their rural
homes and began work in the cotton textile mills? They came to recently
erected factory towns dominated by the textile corporations that owned
much of the land and employed a substantial fraction of the local population. In Lowell in 1840, for instance, textile firms employed more than
8,000 workers, fully 38 percent of the city's population at this date.
Among female residents, this proportion exceeded 47 percent. The mills
themselves were massive five- and six-story structures employing 250 to

---

5. See the family tree, "Sabrina Bennett and her Extended Kinship Network," that appears at the outset of the Sabrina Bennett Letters below.

Boston Manufacturing Company, Waltham, Massachusetts, c. 1826.

Courtesy of Old Sturbridge Village and Lowell Historical Society.

300 workers each. The ten major Lowell firms consisted of thirty-two such mills valued at more than \$10 million in 1840.[6] Across from the mills stood rows of brick boardinghouses for single women and tenements for the families of married men in the work force. Most of the major textile firms in northern New England were owned by a narrow circle of absentee investors known collectively as the Boston Associates. The mills followed a unified set of policies with regard to technology, labor relations, and sales practices, and have been viewed by historians as part of a broader system of textile manufacture, denominated the Waltham-Lowell system.[7]

Mills of the Waltham-Lowell variety shared a number of common elements. Beginning with the innovations promoted by the Boston Manufacturing Company in Waltham in 1814, these firms developed a vertically integrated manufacturing process. Unlike the earlier spinning mills in Rhode Island, they combined all the operations in the manufacture of finished cloth under a single roof. They were not dependent on neighboring farm families for the initial cleaning of the raw cotton or the weaving of the cloth. From the start, these firms used machinery and water power to accomplish the basic carding, spinning, dressing, and weaving steps in the production process. They also established print and dye works and bleacheries to complete the final processing of the finished cloth.

In further contrast to the Rhode Island mills that hired entire families, the Waltham-Lowell firms relied upon a work force comprised chiefly of young, single women, recruited from the neighboring countryside. The composition of the labor force led to additional innovations. The corporations erected boardinghouses to accommodate the recent migrants and established a system of paternalistic regulations to oversee the women while they were employed in the mills. Regulations required women workers, for instance, to be in their boardinghouses by 10:00 each evening and called upon boardinghouse keepers to report violators to the mill management. In the early years, women were required to attend church services regularly, and some mills even deducted pew rent from women's earnings and paid it directly to local churches. These paternalistic controls were aimed at protecting the reputations of women mill

6. *Statistics of Lowell Manufactures,* 1840, 1846, microfilm of annual broadsides available at Baker Library, Harvard Business School.

7. Two works stand out for their treatment of the Waltham-Lowell system: Caroline Ware, *The Early New England Cotton Manufacture: A Study of Industrial Beginnings* (New York: Russell & Russell, 1966, originally published in 1931); and Hannah Josephson, *The Golden Threads: New England's Mill Girls and Magnates* (New York: Duell, Sloan, and Pearce, 1949).

REGULATIONS

FOR THE

BOARDING HOUSES

OF THE

MIDDLESEX COMPANY.

THE tenants of the Boarding Houses are not to board, or permit any part of their houses to be occupied by any person except those in the employ of the Company.

They will be considered answerable for any improper conduct in their houses, and are not to permit their boarders to have company at unseasonable hours.

The doors must be closed at ten o'clock in the evening, and no one admitted after that time without some reasonable excuse.

The keepers of the Boarding Houses must give an account of the number, names, and employment of their boarders, when required; and report the names of such as are guilty of any improper conduct, or are not in the regular habit of attending public worship.

The buildings and yards about them must be kept clean and in good order, and if they are injured otherwise than from ordinary use, all necessary repairs will be made, and charged to the occupant.

It is indispensable that all persons in the employ of the Middlesex Company should be vaccinated who have not been, as also the families with whom they board; which will be done at the expense of the Company.

SAMUEL LAWRENCE, Agent.

JOEL TAYLOR, PRINTER, Daily Courier Office.

Boardinghouse regulations, Middlesex Company, Lowell, Massachusetts, c. 1846.

workers, thus assuring Yankee farmers that they might safely permit their daughters to leave home for factory work. Finally, in contrast to the earlier, smaller spinning mills of southern New England, these firms paid women cash wages on a monthly basis. They only rarely established company stores or issued scrip as their Rhode Island competitors had often done.[8]

The Waltham-Lowell mills revolutionized manufacturing in the years between 1815 and 1850 and set the trend for other industries. These firms contributed to the development and improvement of textile machinery and supported efforts to improve practices in the generation and transmission of waterpower. Furthermore, mill management transformed the organization of production and placed novel demands on the new recruits to the industrial world, the Yankee women workers.

Generally each corporation would erect several large mills, each one a complete and standardized unit of production. During the years that Yankee women were predominant in the work force, the mills were typically four to six stories in height, and perhaps 45 feet wide by 150 feet long. They were constructed of red brick, with regular rows of windows extending along their length and breadth. An outside, enclosed stairway stood along one side, and a bell tower often rose above the roof of the central mill in a given complex.

The bell tower stood as a visible and audible symbol of the new time-discipline ushered in by the Waltham-Lowell factory system. In general, all the mills operated on the same time schedule, with the bells synchronized to ring workers in and out of the mills at set times. In the summer months, for instance, the bells would first wake operatives at 4:30 A.M., so they would be ready for the second bell that called them into the mills at 4:50. Work began ten minutes later and continued until 7:00 when the breakfast bells rang out. Women workers hurried through the mill gates to the boardinghouses that adjoined the mills and could not dally through the meal for the bells would ring them back into the mills at 7:35. They would then work from 7:45 until the bells once again rang them out at noon for a forty-five-minute dinner break. Finally, the bells were silent for a stretch, while the women worked from 12:45 until closing at 7:00 P.M. After supper and a brief evening of visiting, shopping, sewing, or reading, the women turned in at 10:00 P.M., when the mill bells rang out the curfew and boardinghouse keepers were required to close

8. Ware, *Early New England Cotton Manufacture*, chs. 4 and 7; Thomas Dublin, *Women at Work: The Transformation of Work and Community in Lowell, Massachusetts, 1826-1860* (New York: Columbia University Press, 1979), esp. chs. 4 and 5.

Merrimack Company, Lowell, Massachusetts, c. 1850.

TIME TABLE OF THE LOWELL MILLS,

To take effect on and after Oct. 21st, 1851.

The Standard time being that of the meridian of Lowell, as shown by the regulator clock of JOSEPH RAYNES, 43 Central Street

	From 1st to 10th inclusive.				From 11th to 20th inclusive.				From 21st to last day of month.			
	1st Bell	2d Bell	3d Bell	Eve. Bell	1st Bell	2d Bell	3d Bell	Eve. Bell	1st Bell	2d Bell	3d Bell	Eve. Bell
January,	5.00	6.00	6.50	*7.30	5.00	6 00	6.50	*7.30	5.00	6.00	6.50	*7.30
February,	4.30	5.30	6.40	*7.30	4.30	5.30	6.25	*7.30	4.30	5.30	6.15	*7.30
March,	5.40	6.00		*7.30	5.20	5.40		*7.30	5.05	5.25		6.35
April,	4.45	5.05		6.45	4.30	4.50		6.55	4.30	4.50		7.00
May,	4.30	4.50		7·00	4.30	4.50		7.00	4.30	4.50		7 00
June,	"	"		"	"	"		"	"	"		"
July,	"	"		"	"	"		"	"	"		"
August,	"	"		"	"	"		"	"	"		"
September,	4.40	5.00		6.45	4.50	5.10		6.30	5.00	5.20		*7.30
October,	5.10	5.30		*7.30	5.20	5.40		*7.30	5.35	5.55		*7.30
November,	4.30	5.30	6.10	*7.30	4.30	5.30	6.20	*7.30	5.00	6.00	6.35	*7.30
December,	5.00	6.00	6.45	*7.30	5.00	6.00	6.50	*7.30	5.00	6·00	6.50	*7.30

* Excepting on Saturdays from Sept. 21st to March 20th inclusive, when it is rung at 20 minutes after sunset.

YARD GATES,

Will be opened at ringing of last morning bell, of meal bells, and of evening bells; and kept open **Ten minutes.**

MILL GATES.

Commence hoisting Mill Gates, Two minutes before commencing work.

WORK COMMENCES,

At Ten minutes after last morning bell, and at Ten minutes after bell which " rings in " from Meals.

BREAKFAST BELLS.

During March "Ring out".........at....7.30 a. m..........."Ring in" at 8:05 a. m.
April 1st to Sept. 20th inclusive.....at....7 00 " " .... " " at 7.35 " "
Sept. 21st to Oct. 31st inclusive.....at....7.30 " " .... " " at 8.05 " "
Remainder of year work commences after Breakfast.

DINNER BELLS.

" Ring out" .... 12.30 p. m........."Ring in".... 1.05 p. m.

In all cases, the *first* stroke of the bell is considered as marking the time.

Hours of labor in Lowell, 1851.

their doors. No wonder that one character in a mill story complained to her boardinghouse roommates: "Up before day, at the clang of the bell—and out of the mill by the clang of the bell—into the mill, and at work, in obedience to that ding-dong of the bell—just as though we were so many living machines."[9]

Just as the schedules of workers reflected a concern for system and efficiency, the spatial organization of tasks within the mills reflected the new sense of order. The basement housed a waterwheel, purposefully placed below ground level to maximize the power generated and to protect water in the millrace from freezing temperatures. Successive stories housed the carding, spinning, weaving, and dressing steps, each operation occupying a single large room on a floor. An elevator connected the different floors, moving materials from one step in the production process to the next.[10]

Although there were few major technological or organizational breakthroughs in American cotton textile manufacturing between 1830 and 1860, innovations in power transmission permitted a steady increase in the pace of work for women in the mills. In the face of a highly competitive market for cloth goods, Waltham-Lowell firms made strenuous efforts to reduce their unit labor costs. By assigning increasing numbers of machines to workers without raising wages, the firms managed to reduce labor costs and maintain profits in the face of declining prices for their cloth. At the Hamilton Company in Lowell, for instance, the average number of looms per weaver increased from 1.3 to 2.9 in the years between 1840 and 1854, two points in time for which we have particularly reliable data. The workload for spinners increased by an almost identical proportion. And the Hamilton figures are not an isolated example. For this same period the average number of spindles per millhand increased by about 64 percent for the eight leading textile firms in Lowell. Despite the gains in productivity, average wages for women declined slightly in these years.[11]

The wages and hours of labor for women in the early mills strike most late twentieth-century observers as almost unbelievable. Women in the

9. *Time Table of the Lowell Mills*, Oct. 1851, Baker Library, Harvard Business School; "The Spirit of Discontent," *The Lowell Offering*, (1841), 1:113. For a broader discussion of the cultural conflicts that ensued with the imposition of this new work-discipline, see E.P. Thompson, "Time, Work-Discipline, and Industrial Capitalism," *Past and Present* (1967), no. 38, pp. 56-97.
10. Henry Miles, *Lowell As It Was and As It Is* (Lowell: Powers and Bagley, 1845), pp. 76-84; James Montgomery, *A Practical Detail of the Cotton Manufacture of the United States of America* (Glasgow, Scotland: John Niven, 1840), p. 16.
11. Dublin, *Women at Work*, pp. 137, 161.

mid-1830s, for instance, earned about $3.25 for a seventy-three-hour work week—a wage under five cents per hour.[12] And yet, thousands of women left their rural homes and came to Lowell, Nashua, and other mill towns, glad to earn wages on this scale. But, if these wages appear incredibly low, so too were prices of necessities. Room and board in company boardinghouses cost only $1.25 per week, leaving women a surplus of about $2.00 a week. These wages compared favorably with earnings in domestic service, teaching, or sewing, three of the major alternatives open to women in these years.[13] And, although the work week called for six twelve-hour days in the mills, this schedule was not very different from what women were used to on the farm. Certainly the pace of the machinery placed more demands on women than did domestic chores on the farm, but the dawn-to-dusk schedule was not new. The only practice that many found disturbing was the evening work in the winter when women continued to labor by oil lamps until six or seven o'clock.

Under pressure from organized women workers, the textile firms reduced the hours of labor. In 1847 an extension of the dinner hour cut the working day to eleven and a half hours and in 1853 a second reduction resulted in a work week of sixty-six hours, an average of eleven hours each day. The increasing pace of work in the mills necessitated these reforms, for when workers tended four looms instead of two or experienced a similar increase in the number of spindles, it proved almost impossible to maintain a reasonable level of efficiency for a twelve-hour day. Even with this reduction in the hours of labor, the daily output of workers expanded without interruption.[14]

It is difficult for us as twentieth-century observers to enter the world of the textile mills of the mid-nineteenth century. Still, we must make the imaginative effort, and in so doing try to view this world from the perspective of the young rural women who comprised such a large proportion of the mill work force. To do so it will help to shift our vision from the mills themselves and consider at least briefly the farming experiences the women had before they entered the mills. The most important characteristic of New England farming at the turn of the nineteenth century was that it provided work for all members of the family throughout the year. Men worked in the fields, transported and marketed farm products, and handled repairs and construction. Women took care of poultry and

12. *Statistics of Lowell Manufactures,* 1836.
13. For a view of the relative earnings of teachers and mill operatives, see Richard M. Bernard and Maris Vinovskis, "The Female School Teacher in Ante-Bellum Massachusetts," *Journal of Social History* (1977), 10:332-45.
14. For a fuller treatment of these reductions in hours and of the labor struggles that led to them, see Dublin, *Women at Work,* chs. 7 and 12.

dairy stock, made such salable products as butter, cheese, brooms, yarn, and cloth, and provided food and clothing for family consumption and use. The efficiency of the family farm stemmed from its concentration on the production of secondary goods for the seaboard market. This meant that members of farming families raised crops in season and then processed these raw materials or fed them to livestock for subsequent use or sale.[15]

The years between 1790 and 1808 saw the expansion of agriculture in northern New England onto marginal farming lands of the rocky hill country. Increasing demand for foodstuffs in coastal cities and the growth of exports to meet European demand during the years of the Napoleonic Wars encouraged an expansion that lacked a solid foundation. The decline of exports to Europe that came with the enactment of the Embargo and Non-Intercourse Acts undermined the short-lived prosperity. Farmers found themselves overextended and were hard-pressed to meet mortgage obligations. As markets shrank and prices of agricultural products declined, farmers found it difficult to make a living on the less productive marginal hill lands they had purchased.

While many farmers felt the loss of the export trade, others were able to shift their production to meet the needs of the growing urban market. Between 1810 and 1860 the proportion of New Englanders living in cities with populations greater than 10,000 increased from 7 to 36 percent. This growth in the urban population contributed to the rise of specialized commercial agriculture in the areas adjoining cities.[16]

Improvements in inland transportation further stimulated commerical agriculture by widening the area of farming within which products could easily be brought to market. However, since these improvements were not confined to New England their impact was contradictory. Canals, toll roads, and later railroads did widen the circle of profitable specialized production of milk and perishables for urban markets. But these same improvements, by decreasing long-haul freight rates from the West, made it possible for farmers in newly settled areas to compete within eastern markets. Wheat and dairy products from New York and wheat and wool from Ohio, Indiana, and Illinois spelled disaster for farmers on marginal hill-country land.[17]

15. Henry Bass Hall, "A Description of Rural Life and Labor at Four Periods" (Ph.D. diss., Harvard University, 1918), p. 103.
16. Percy Bidwell, "The Agricultural Revolution in New England," in L.B. Schmidt and E.A. Ross, eds., *Readings in the Economic History of American Agriculture* (New York: Macmillan, 1925), p. 237.
17. George Rogers Taylor, *The Transportation Revolution, 1815-1860* (New York: Harper and Row, 1951), chs. 7 and 8.

The increasing proportion of New Englanders residing in cities created an urban market for various foodstuffs grown in the surrounding countryside. Farmers fed the city-dwellers, but at the same time they provided a share of the raw materials processed by urban industry. In particular, the expansion of woolen textiles in these years stimulated farmers to shift much of their land to pasturage and to increase the size of their flocks of sheep. Prosperous herders bought up the lands of neighbors, and the number of sheep in each of the northern New England states peaked in 1840. Farmers in Maine, New Hampshire, and Vermont together owned 3 million sheep in 1840. Vermonters led the way with about 1.7 million sheep, almost six for each inhabitant. Although the sale of wool to Massachusetts mills benefited farmers, the expansion of pastures devoured family farms and reduced the demand for agricultural laborers, hence contributing to the rising tide of emigration out of northern New England in the 1830s.[18]

The growth of textile production contributed to migration in yet another way. The expansion of the factory output of cotton and woolen cloth undermined the position of women in farming families. Before 1820 spinning and weaving had been the primary domestic occupations of farmers' daughters. But with the expanded output of the new mills the home production of cloth became increasingly unprofitable. The prices of coarse cloths fell to one-sixth of former values and families quickly substituted store-bought fabrics for homespun. In this manner, they lost the income that the household production of cloth had at times provided and they soon gave up supplying their own domestic needs as well. A contemporary spokesman decried the social consequences of this development:

> It is a deceptive and dangerous economy, which induces a farmer to buy all the woolens of the manufacturer, merely because he can buy them cheap— cheaper even than he supposes he can make them at home. . . . While the farmer is buying at the store, what he could make at home . . . the members of his family . . . are unemployed, or employed to little or no purpose.

As daughters in farming families found themselves without this domestic occupation, they looked elsewhere for employment and a sense of usefulness. For a fair number of women New England's mill towns offered an appealing alternative.[19]

18. Harold F. Wilson, *The Hill Country of Northern New England* (New York: Columbia University Press, 1936), ch. 4; Lewis Stilwell, *Migration from Vermont* (Montpelier: Vermont Historical Society, 1948), pp. 157-58, 172-73.
19. Rolla Tryon, *Household Manufactures in the United States, 1640-1860: A Study in Industrial History* (Chicago: University of Chicago Press, 1917), pp. 271 ff.; the quote is from Bidwell, "Agricultural Revolution," p. 246.

The predominant response to the dramatic changes of this period was the migration of young men and women from northern New England. Increasingly, the sons and daughters of New Hampshire and Vermont farmers left the homestead, heading to cheaper, more fertile lands in the West or seeking employment in the expanding cities and mill towns of central and southern New England. The women whose letters are included in this book were participants in this migration. Sarah Hodgdon left Rochester, New Hampshire to work in the Lowell mills, and her sister, Elizabeth, taught school in South Berwick, Maine and Great Falls, New Hampshire. Mary Paul, from Barnard, Vermont, migrated numerous times, living in Massachusetts, New Hampshire, Vermont, New Jersey, and New Hampshire again, before finally settling in Lynn, Massachusetts. Delia Page did not leave her native state when she entered the Manchester, New Hampshire mills, but after marriage she and her husband headed for California. The restless spirit evident in these young women was typical of their generation.

There had been a steady movement of migrants out of Vermont and New Hampshire since 1800, but 1830 marked the beginning of a flood that dwarfed the earlier trickle. Between 1800 and 1830 the population of Vermont, for instance, increased by more than 80 percent. Thereafter, emigration reduced this rate of growth, and over the next three decades Vermont's overall population rose only 12 percent. No more than a small part of this slowdown in growth can be attributed to a declining birthrate. In 1850, 146,000 Vermont natives resided in other states. By 1860, this number increased still further to 175,000, fully 42 percent of all the Vermont-born enumerated in that census. The flow of migrants out of the state was spreading Vermonters throughout the nation.[20]

Where did these migrants go? The largest numbers headed west, with New York, Ohio, Illinois, Michigan and Wisconsin taking large shares of Vermont natives in 1850. Massachusetts was a strong second, after New York, accounting for 12 percent of Vermont natives living in other states.[21] The net urban stream was much smaller than the westward flow, but it had an importance far greater than is evident from the statistics alone. Many of those who worked in the cities returned to their native towns or migrated west, and the figures from the 1850 census understate the total number of rural natives who at some point in their lives experienced the urban, industrial setting.

This migration transformed not only the countryside, but the urban setting as well. Rural migrants comprised a significant proportion of resi-

20. Stilwell, *Migration from Vermont*, pp. 95, 171n, 214-16.
21. Stilwell, *Migration from Vermont*, p. 214.

dents in many New England cities. In Boston, for instance, about 12 percent of residents enumerated in the 1850 census had been born in New Hampshire, Maine, or Vermont. These recent migrants, most of them in their 20s and 30s, undoubtedly comprised a much larger proportion of the work force than that 12 percent would indicate. An extreme example of this concentration is evident in Lowell, where natives of northern New England made up more than three-fourths of all women workers in the mills in 1845.[22]

The transformation of agriculture in northern New England between 1790 and 1850 promoted migration to the growing mill towns in these decades. Still, it may be useful to move from this level of generalization to ask two more specific questions: who, after all, were the women who left their farming homes to enter the New England mills, and what individual motivations prompted their actions? These two questions can be restated in another way: how were the broader forces affecting New England agriculture felt in the daily lives of those farmers' daughters who chose mill employment?

To answer these questions it is helpful to consider individual women within specific rural communities. One might focus on those women who have left letters, diaries, or reminiscences, but their numbers are too few to give any assurance of their representativeness. The records of the antebellum textile corporations offer a way around this difficulty. Most of the larger textile firms kept records of workers' entrances into and departures from the labor force, noting their former rural residences. In earlier research I traced 175 women from three New Hampshire communities—Boscawen, Canterbury, and Sutton—who worked at the Hamilton Manufacturing Company in Lowell, Massachusetts between 1830 and 1850. Using a variety of sources I traced these women back to their families and forward to their marriages after mill employment. The findings of this study provide a context within which to place the letter writers included in this volume.[23]

Judging from this group of women workers, millhands came from the middle ranks of rural farming families. Examining the tax inventories of their parents, we find their families underrepresented among both the very poor and the very rich in their hometowns. They were, however, less well off on the average than families of young women who remained

22. Miles, *Lowell As It Was and As It Is*, p. 193; J.D.B. Debow, *Statistical View of the United States* (Washington, 1854), p. 399.
23. Hamilton Manufacturing Company Records, vols. 481-500, Baker Library, Harvard Business School. For a fuller discussion of method, see Dublin, *Women at Work*, app. 2.

at home. The median property holding of the families of nonmigrant women from Boscawen, Canterbury, and Sutton was $680 in 1830, twice the figure of $338 for families of these millhands.[24]

What data we have on the family origins of women mill workers suggest that they came from lesser propertied farming families in northern New England. Absolute impoverishment was not a problem; still, mill employment may have served a number of economic needs for women and their families. First, the women came from large families, averaging more than seven children, and a daughter's departure for the mills meant one less person to feed and perhaps some reduction in overcrowding at home. Second, mill earnings may have provided women with a marriage portion, and thus would have reduced the demands on a family's limited property. In this way employment provided women with immediate support while permitting them to save for their future needs.

Quantitative evidence, while helpful in placing broad parameters on the economic backgrounds of operatives, does not really probe individual motivations. We might view the economic standing of families as a factor predisposing daughters to enter the mills, but what more immediate motivations prompted individual women? In this regard personal letters provide particularly rich insights into the values and attitudes that led women to take up mill employment.[25]

The letter writers included in this collection offer views that expand upon the evidence presented here. Mary Paul, of Barnard, Vermont, began work in the Lowell mills at the age of fifteen, in November 1845. Before going to the mills she had worked briefly as a domestic servant and then lived with relatives a short distance from her home; at that time she wrote seeking her father's permission to go to Lowell. Here she revealed the basic motivation that prompted her request: "I think it would be much better for me [in Lowell] than to stay about here. . . . I am in need of clothes which I cannot get about here and for that reason I want to go to Lowell or some other place." After getting permission, Mary Paul worked off and on in Lowell for at least four years. In 1850 she lived

24. For purposes of comparison I have drawn a group of nonmigrant couples whose marriages were recorded in published genealogies of the three towns. For inclusion in this group, one member of the couple had to be born between 1805 and 1825 and neither member (nor any siblings) could have migrated to, married an individual from, or given birth to children in a New England mill town or city. Dublin, *Women at Work*, p. 35; see also Thomas Dublin, "The Social Origins and Social Consequences of Urban Migration," unpublished paper presented at the annual meeting of the Social Science History Association, November 1979.

25. The following pages are closely based on the evidence and argument presented in Dublin, *Women at Work*, ch. 3.

briefly with her father, but then went on her own again, this time working as a seamstress in Brattleboro, Vermont. She evidently felt some guilt at not contributing to her father's support. In an 1853 letter she wrote "I hope sometime to be able to do something for you and sometimes feel ashamed that I have not before this." She evidently was not contributing anything from her earnings toward her father's support as she noted her inability to "lay up" any savings after meeting her normal living expenses. She expressed the wish that sometime she could live with her father and perhaps provide for him but always fell back on the argument that sent her to Lowell in the first place: "I . . . must work where I can get more pay."[26]

Sally Rice of Somerset, Vermont, not included among the letter writers in this volume, left her home in 1838 at the age of seventeen to take her first job "working out." She went first to Union Village, New York, where she supported herself on farm labor, and then moved to Thompson, Connecticut, where she found employment in a textile factory. That she was working for her own personal support and not to assist her family is evident in a poignant letter she wrote to her parents from Union Village in 1839 rejecting her familial home:

> I never can be happy there in among so many mountains. I feel as tho I have worn out shoes and strenth enough riding and walking over the mountains. I think it would be more consistent to save my strength to raise my boys. . . . I shall need all I have got and as for marrying and settling in that wilderness I wont. And if a person ever expects to take comfort it is while they are young. . . . I have got so that by next summer if I could stay I would begin to lay up something. . . . I am now most 19 years old. I must of course have something of my own before many more years have passed over my head and where is that something coming from if I go home and earn nothing. . . . You may think me unkind but how can you blame me for wanting to stay here. I have but one life to live and I want to enjoy myself as well as I can while I live.[27]

Sally Rice wanted to earn "something of my own," which was obviously not possible in the family economy of her father's farm. The more fertile lands of neighboring New York created a demand for agricultural

26. Mary Paul to Bela Paul, Sept. 13, 1845, Nov. 27, 1853, Dec. 18, 1853, see below.
27. Sally Rice to Hazelton and Rhoda Rice, Union Village, 1839, Dover Free Library, East Dover, Vermont. Edited selections from this collection will appear in *The New England Mill Village*, vol. 2 in *Documents in American Industrial History*, Michael Brewster Folsom, general editor (forthcoming, M.I.T. Press). My thanks to Michael Folsom for sharing his transcriptions while still in manuscript.

labor and offered wages high enough to attract Sally Rice away from the "wilderness" about Somerset. The higher wages in textile mills soon lured this farmer's daughter to Thompson, Connecticut. Earning wages to provide for a dowry seems to have been Sally Rice's primary motivation for leaving home in 1838. She was, after all, concerned to earn money and to "save my strength to raise my boys," though she was eighteen and unmarried and any boys were as yet unborn. Mill employment appealed to her principally because its wages were higher than those for farm laborers or domestic servants. She did not consider mill work a long-term prospect, but intended to remain there only briefly: "I should not like to spend my days in a mill . . . unless they are short because I like a Farm too well for that." Finally, in 1847, probably with a sufficient dowry laid up, Sally Rice married the brother of a fellow operative and settled in Worcester, Massachusetts.[28]

If clothes and a dowry provided the motivation for Mary Paul and Sally Rice to leave home and work in textile factories, a desire for education stimulated the efforts of a mill worker in Clinton, Massachusetts in 1851. One Lucy Ann had her sights set on attending Oberlin College. In a letter to a cousin she wrote: "I have earned enough to school me awhile, & have not I a right to do so, or must I go home, like a dutiful girl, place the money in father's hands, & then there goes all my hard earnings." If she had to turn her wages over to her family she would consider them a "dead loss," and all her efforts would have been "spent in vain." Clearly, mill employment could be turned to individualistic purposes. As Lucy Ann summed up her thinking: "I merely wish to go [to Oberlin] because I think it the best way of spending the money I have worked so hard to earn."[29]

Lucy Ann evidently felt a need to justify her actions. A tone of defensiveness creeps into her language here, but other mill letters reveal that it was often taken for granted, by operatives and parents alike, that women's earnings were their own to spend as they pleased. Consider an 1840 letter, included in the first collection below, from Elizabeth Hodgdon to her sister, Sarah, working in the mills of nearby Great Falls:

> You say you want to come home when we all think you have staid long enough, but we do not know better than you or so well either when you

28. Sally Rice to Hazelton Rice, Masonville, Feb. 23, 1845. For brief excerpts from these letters and discussions of the Rice family background see Nell Kull, ed., " 'I Can Never Be Happy In There Among So Many Mountains': The Letters of Sally Rice," *Vermont History* (1970), 38:49-57.

29. Loriman Brigham, "An Independent Voice: A Mill Girl from Vermont Speaks Her Mind," *Vermont History* (1973), 41:144.

have earned as much as you will want to spend. Yet it is Mothers opinion
& mine that you have already as much as you will probably want to spend
if you lay it out to good advantage which we doubt not but you will.[30]

Elizabeth suggests, and her mother evidently concurs, that Sarah
should work as long as necessary to earn what she felt she needed. When
Sarah returned home it is likely that she did not turn her savings over to
her parents, but spent them as she chose. The earnings undoubtedly
relieved her parents of certain expenses they might have incurred had
she simply lived at home, and in this way her income was a help to them.
These lines reinforce the distinct impression that emerges from the letters as a whole—when daughters left home and entered the mills they
ceased to be "dependents" in the traditional sense. They supported
themselves while at work and used their savings to maintain a certain
independence even when they lived at home.

The Hodgdon correspondence is important because it suggests that
there was no great conflict between familial and individual interests for
most women workers. Parents gave their approval to daughters' plans to
work in the mills and were glad to see them earning money for themselves. Times were often hard in northern New England after 1830, and
even in prosperous years there were limited opportunities for women to
earn anything while living at home. With the growth of factory textile
production, the contributions of farmers' daughters to the family economy declined significantly. Furthermore, each departure meant one less
mouth to feed. Eben Jennison of Charleston, Maine may have reflected
the changing calculus of the family economy when, in 1849, he wrote to
a daughter who was working in Lowell: "The season with us has been
verry Dry and the Drough[t] verry severe. The crops are very light indeed and business verry Dull. If you should be blessed with your health
and are contented I think you will do better where you are than you
could do here." For Jennison, these years appear to have been difficult
ones, and by 1858 he had two daughters employed in the mills. In one of
his letters to them he acknowledged the receipt of five dollars and expressed the hope that "some day or other" he would be able to repay
them "with interest." Throughout his correspondence to his daughters, it
is clear that he felt they should be in Lowell, but not because he expected
them to contribute to his support as a matter of course. In fact his pride
and sense of self-respect made it difficult for him to accept their apparently unsolicited aid, although need won out in the end. Even as he took

30. Elizabeth Hodgdon to Sarah Hodgdon, March 29, 1840, see below.

their money he viewed it as a loan to be repaid when his economic fortunes had improved.[31]

The view of women's motivations that emerges from analysis of their social origins and of their correspondence stands in sharp contrast to contemporary published writing that stressed the selfless contributions of working women to their families. Stories and essays in *The Lowell Offering*, an operatives' literary magazine, contended that entirely unselfish motives led women to enter the mills. Characters in "factory tales" were invariably orphans supporting themselves and younger siblings, young women working to pay off the mortgage on the family farm or to send a brother to college, or widows providing for their children. Never in the fiction did an operative work simply to buy new clothes, pay for her own continued education, or save for some other individual purpose. These writers are not entirely trustworthy, however, for they were engaged in a heated "factory controversy," and their writings were intended to show the moral uprightness and selflessness of their fellow operatives. The private letters of mill workers are far more believable than the published showpieces.[32]

Mill work should not be viewed as simply an extension of the traditional family economy as work for women moved outside the home. Work in the mills functioned for women rather like migration did for young men who could see that their chances of setting up on a farm in an established rural community were rather slim. The mills offered individual self-support, enabled women to enjoy urban amenities not available in their rural communities, and gave them a measure of economic and social independence from their families. These factors made the new factory towns attractive to rural women. The steady movement of the family farm from a subsistence to a commercial basis made daughters relatively "expendable" and gave fathers who otherwise might have guarded the family labor supply reason to allow them a chance on their own.

The work patterns in Lowell are strikingly different from those evident for young, single European women in this period. Recent historians have argued that women's work outside the home in nineteenth-century Europe was basically an adaptaion of the traditional family economy within

31. Eben Jennison Letters, Sept. 2, 1849, July 13, 1858. Courtesy of Harry and Mary Dinmore, Lowell, Mass.
32. *The Lowell Offering*, 1:161-71, 2:145-55, 246-50. For more on the broader controversy itself, see Norman Ware, *The Industrial Worker, 1840-1860: The Reaction of American Industrial Society to the Advance of the Industrial Revolution* (Gloucester, Mass.: Peter Smith, 1959), ch. 5.

a changed economic setting. Within this view, a "daughter working as a servant, seamstress, or factory operative became an arm of the family economy, and arrangements were made to ensure her contribution even though she did not live at home."[33] Similar practices prevailed earlier in spinning mills in southern New England that hired entire families, but they were never the dominant pattern in mill towns of the Waltham-Lowell variety. Operatives' correspondence suggests that most women spent and saved their earnings as they chose, with little pressure to contribute to the support of their families.

Several factors are relevant in explaining the differences in the American setting. First, the family economy in rural New England differed from its counterpart among European peasants. Diaries of American women suggest that daughters living at home often kept a portion of their earnings, indicating that even then they were not totally subordinated within the family economy.[34] Second, as New England daughters sought mill employment they generally left home and accepted a considerable separation from their families, in terms of both distance and time. This physical separation and the women's residence in a peer-group community of other young, single women further encouraged their economic and social independence. Finally, their correspondence suggests they did not encounter very strong parental pressures in this regard. Parents encouraged their daughters, or at least appear to have given their approval, and did not expect that they would place their earnings in the family till. Joan Scott and Louise Tilly point out that over time "more individualistic and instrumental" attitudes did develop among European working women, but these attitudes appear to have developed more rapidly and with less resistance in New England than in the European context.[35]

Although single migrant women predominated in the textile mills of northern New England in the antebellum years, there were a number of workers who resided with their families in the mill towns. For the Hamilton Company in Lowell, for instance, about 11 percent of women employed in July 1836 resided with their families while working. By 1860, this proportion had reached 35 percent. In smaller mill towns the propor-

33. Joan Scott and Louise Tilly, *Women, Work, and Family* (New York: Holt, Rinehart and Winston, 1978), pp. 109, 115-16.

34. Blanche Brown Bryant and Gertrude Elaine Baker, eds., *The Diaries of Sally and Pamela Brown* (Springfield, Vt.: William L. Bryant Foundation, 1970), Feb. 11, 1832, May 31, Oct. 30, Nov. 7, Dec. 2 and 7, 1833, Nov. 3, Dec. 5, 1837.

35. Scott and Tilly, "Women's Work and the Family in Nineteenth-Century Europe," *Comparative Studies in Society and History* (1975), 17:61-62. See also their *Women, Work, and Family*, pp. 116-21.

tion of workers living with their families was often even higher. In Webster, Massachusetts in 1850, more than 55 percent of mill workers in one of the Slater mills resided with their families.[36]

Surviving reminiscences of former mill women and parental letters indicate that these workers were definitely contributing to immediate family income. Chief among family workers were sons and daughters of boardinghouse keepers. Harriet Hanson Robinson and Lucy Larcom began work as bobbin girls in the Lowell mills at age ten or eleven. Both their families had moved to Lowell upon the death of a father, and children's mill earnings provided a crucial addition to the income of widowed mothers. Late in their lives, both women recalled their desires to assist their families. Robinson recorded in her reminiscences: "I wanted to earn *money* like the other little girls." Larcom, recalling adult relatives discussing whether she and her sister would enter the mills, remembered "fearing that I should not be permitted to do the coveted work." For both girls work signaled their growing responsibility to and importance within their families.[37]

Among the letter writers included in this book, Jemima Sanborn provides a parental perspective on a similar situation. She described her motivation for moving with her family to the mill town of Nashua in 1843:

You will probely want to know the cause of our moveing here which are many. I will menshion afew of them. One of them is the hard times to get a living off the farm for so large a famely so we have devided our famely for this year. We have left Plummer and Luther to care for the farm and granmarm and Aunt Polly. The rest of us have moved to Nashvill [a part of Nashua] thinking the girls and Charles they would probely work in the Mill. But we have had bad luck in giting them in only Jane has got in yet. Ann has the promis of going to the mill next week. Hannah is going to school. We are in hopes to take a few borders but have not got any yet.[38]

This Yankee mother moved to a mill town with three daughters and a son for the express purpose of improving the family economic stituation. Jemima Sanborn expected to combine children's wages and income from boarders. Like the European parents described by Tilly and Scott, she

36. Dublin, *Women at Work*, pp. 27, 166; Jonathan Prude, "The Coming of Industrial Order: A Study of Town and Factory Life in Rural Massachusetts, 1813-1860" (Ph.D. diss., Harvard University, 1976), p. 326.
37. Robinson, *Loom and Spindle; or Life Among the Early Mill Girls* (New York: Thomas Y. Crowell, 1898), p. 30; Larcom, *A New England Girlhood* (Boston: Houghton Mifflin, 1889), p. 153.
38. Jemima Sanborn to Richard and Ruth Bennett, May 14, 1843, see below.

undoubtedly sent her daughters into the mills to contribute to family income. Unlike the situations of Sarah Hodgdon or Mary Paul, here we see an example of a "family wage economy."

Similar strategies are evident in a letter written by Vermonter Gardner Plimpton from the mill town of Whitinsville, Massachusetts in 1847. In his letter, not included below, Plimpton tried to persuade a friend to bring his family down as well. "I do no[t] know how your are situated," he wrote, "but I think you can live here eas[i]er and make more money here then up thare." He went on to list the new opportunities:

> You take some Borders, the children work in the mill, you can have steady work all the time and good wages if you are well. You[r] incum will at least bee six hundred Dollars a year. . . . I wish you to come down this winter and see me and look around an see if it is not best. Fore it is hard bisness for a poor man up thare.

Plimpton was sold on the family labor system. As he noted to his friend, "I would not go back to vermont to live as I did the last two or three years."[39]

These letters indicate that while the vast majority of mill women left their families behind when they entered the textile factories, for a distinct minority mill work remained fully integrated within the family economy. Still, even those women who left their families to enter wage labor did not do so as isolated individuals but as members of broader kin networks. Almost two-thirds of women workers traced from the Hamilton Company in Lowell back to their homes in central New Hampshire had relatives also employed at the same firm between 1830 and 1850.[40] The letters reprinted here reinforce this quantitative evidence but demonstrate that if we broaden our vision beyond the limits of a single firm the extent of kinship networks was greater still. Of all the women workers included among these letter writers only Delia Page, who was estranged from her immediate family, did not either live or work with relatives at some point during her mill career.

The women's letters are instructive on this note. Sarah Hodgdon of Rochester, New Hampshire offers a case in point. She came to Lowell with two friends from her hometown, Wealthy Page and Elizabeth. Wealthy was older and had previously worked in Lowell, and she assisted the newcomers in the difficulties of their first months. The three

---

39. Gardner Plimpton to Werden Babcock, Jan. 10, 1847, Vermont Historical Society.
40. Dublin, *Women at Work*, p. 42.

young women lived together and worked in the same weaving room. Sarah felt ill-treated by members of her church, apparently because she could not afford to rent a pew. Wealthy Page stood by her during this crisis, writing in a letter back to Rochester: "I am just the same friend to Sarah that I was when I promised to befriend her."[41] How long Sarah worked in Lowell is unclear, but in 1840 she was working at the Great Falls Manufacturing Company in New Hampshire. Sister Elizabeth wrote to her at this date, but may have see her often as well, for she taught in the district schools in Great Falls during these years.[42] When single women left their own homes in the mid-nineteenth century they often did so in the company of a sister or some other female relative.

The Hodgdon correspondence presents us with only the simplest form of continuing family ties among women mill workers. The experience of members of the Sawyer family offers a fuller picture of possibilities. In the letters from Louisa and Olive Sawyer to their cousin, Sabrina Bennett, it becomes clear that five of the seven children in this family worked in Lowell at some point between 1835 and 1850. Hepzibah, Louisa, and Emeline all worked in Lowell off and on over the course of these years. Brothers Daniel and Jeremiah also worked there; in fact, Jeremiah died there in October 1840. In addition, a cousin, Lafayette Frisbie, worked in Lowell for a short period in 1845.[43]

Sabrina Bennett received a steady stream of letters from distant cousins and aunts, including ones from numerous relatives living in the mill town of Nashua, New Hampshire. Persis Edwards and her aunt, Malenda Edwards, worked there and boarded together in 1839. Between 1843 and 1845 Malenda was back in Nashua, living this time with her married sister, Jemima Edwards Sanborn. Several of Jemima's children also worked in the mills, as did Persis's younger brother James. The Sanborn household represented a nexus for an extensive kinship network that is strikingly revealed in letters to Sabrina Bennett.

The correspondence of Mary Paul, the third set of letters reprinted here, reinforces the picture of kinship bonds that emerges in the other letters. When Mary Paul was about to leave for Lowell in November 1845 she asked her father and brothers to come down to her aunt's home to see her off. In letters written from Lowell she repeatedly suggested that her brothers might come and work in the city. Initially her letters were

41. Wealthy Page to "Respected friends," June 6, 1830, see below.
42. For Elizabeth Hodgdon's school employment see Sanborn Family Papers, MHS. See also her accounts of earnings and expenses below.
43. Lafayette Frisbie to Sabrina Bennett, April 20, May 9, 1845, Bennett Family Letters, but not reprinted below.

not persuasive and she remained the only family member in Lowell. She had support, however, as two sisters from her hometown, Mercy and Luthera Griffith, accompanied her to Lowell and helped her find her first job. Her younger brother Henry did ultimately work at the Lowell Machine Shop, at least between 1853 and 1855, although his work does not appear to have overlapped with Mary's.[44]

Kinship ties among mill operatives played a number of important roles for women workers in early Lowell. The existence of these bonds must have eased the shock of adjustment both to work in the factories and to the novel urban setting. Many pairs of sisters or cousins employed by the Hamilton Company in Lowell resided together in company boarding-houses and worked in the same rooms of the mill. The Sawyer sisters and Persis and Malenda Edwards provide two examples. These networks would have been particularly important for newcomers. Experienced operatives helped newcomers by arranging for housing accommodations ahead of time and by lining up jobs with an overseer. Julia A. Dutton, of Clintonville, Massachusetts, described the arrangements she had made for a sister in an 1847 letter to her mother in Vermont:

> I have engaged a place for Martha Coffren the first of Nov[ember]. The overseer sayed she might come at that [date] and if she is large enough for a weaver he will take her if not she can go into some other room. There is no doubt but she will work a plenty.[45]

The presence of an older, more knowledgeable family member in Lowell must have comforted parents thinking about allowing a second child to make the journey. An 1849 letter from Eben Jennison of Charleston, Maine to his daughter, Elizabeth, in Lowell, made this point explicitly. Referring to a younger daughter, then sixteen, he noted:

> A few words in relation to Emily. She has got about ready to come to Lowel. Martha A. Marshall expects to return to Lowel in the course of some two or three weeks and if Emily comes she will come with hir. I should not consent to hir coming at any rate if you was not there. She is young and needs a mothers care and a mothers advise. You must se to hir and give hir such council as you thinks she needs. She may be Homesick for a spell but if you comfort hir up she will soon get the better of it.[46]

---

44. For the Griffith sisters see Mary Paul to Bela Paul, Sept. 13, 1845, Nov. 20, 1845, below. For Henry Paul, see *Lowell City Directory*, 1853-1855.
45. Julia Dutton to Lucretia Dutton, Sept. 26, 1847, Dutton Family Letters. Courtesy of Aileen Eurich, Waitsfield, Vt.
46. Eben Jennison to Elizabeth Jennison, Sept. 2, 1849.

Since most of the women were in their teens when they first set off for the mills, family ties must have been a comfort for both the operatives and their parents.

The close, supportive relations among sisters, cousins, or friends in mill boardinghouses paralleled the experiences of young women in the boarding schools of this period. Carroll Smith-Rosenberg and Nancy Cott, examining letters and diaries of somewhat wealthier women, found much the same sense of mutual affection and "sisterhood" among students at private academies. Even though class shaped the specific experiences of these two groups of women, their letters reveal important areas in which shared gender appears to have outweighed class differences.[47]

This family support network helped operatives adjust to the demands of urban life, but it also made a more direct contribution to women's success in the mills. Of the Hamilton millhands traced back to their hometowns in New Hampshire, those women with other kin working at the firm were able, on the whole, to secure better jobs in the mills. More than 70 percent of women with relatives in the work force were hired initially to work in the high-paying weaving and dressing rooms, while only 52 percent of those without relatives did as well. A consequence of this better job placement for newcomers with kin was that they remained longer at the company. Those with relatives worked at Hamilton an average of 3.7 years; those without kin remained only 2.2 years. Thus, in terms of both earnings and length of careers, women who were part of a family support system enjoyed advantages over those who came to the mills entirely on their own.[48]

When family members were unable to live together in mill towns, women mill workers felt strongly their separation from friends and family. Sarah Hodgdon's first letter home poignantly expressed the continuing bond that tied mill women to their families. It closed: "Give my love to my farther tell him not to forget me and to my dear sister and to my brothers and to my grammother tell her I do not forget her and to my Aunts and to all my enquiring friends." Her feelings welled into homesickness in a poem that closed a subsequent letter:

> I want to se[e] you more I think
> Than I can write with pen and ink.
> But when I shall I cannot tell
> But from my heart I wish you well.

47. Smith-Rosenberg, "The Female World of Love and Ritual: Relations Between Women in Nineteenth-Century America," *Signs* (1976) 1:19; Cott, *Bonds of Womanhood*, pp. 176-77.
48. Dublin, *Women at Work*, pp. 48-49.

I wish you well from all my heart
Although we are so far apart.
If you die there and I die here,
Before one God we shall apeare.[49]

All the evidence suggests that women workers in the early mills were part of a social network of family and friends which had its roots in the countryside and which played an important role in their lives in the mill towns. While women may not have been working expressly to contribute to their families back home, they were still operating within a familial context that is best viewed as a part of their traditional rural culture. Mill employment had not recast women within a completely individualistic mold. Women continued to provide crucial support to one another, as neighbors and family members had done for years in the countryside. They recruited one another into the mills, secured jobs for each other, and helped newcomers make the numerous adjustments called for in a very new and different setting. This is clear evidence of traditional kinds of social relationships serving new purposes.

An understanding of the social origins of women mill workers and of the kinship and friendship networks that they brought with them into the mills helps to place their experience within a broader New England framework. We do well, however, to try to place the experience more clearly within the life cycle of mill women. We may ask in this regard a number of related questions. First, at what age did women start work in the New England textile mills, and for how long did they remain? Second, what difference did this experience make in their later lives? Did mill employment significantly influence their later lives, or was it simply a brief and rather inconsequential episode? To answer these questions we must examine the experiences of specific women.

One way to look at these issues is to trace the various letter writers in this volume and summarize their experiences in something approaching a collective biography. Ann Blake, Louisa Sawyer, and Mary Paul provide examples that suggest the range of career possibilities. Ann Blake began work at the Jackson Company in Nashua in 1843 at the age of fifteen. After only a summer in the mill she commenced working for a dressmaker, a trade she followed in Nashua for at least two years. By 1850 she was still unmarried, boarding in Concord, New Hampshire and working in a shop. In 1853, after supporting herself for ten years, she married William Lovejoy and probably gave up paid employment. Her

49. Sarah Hodgdon to Mary Hodgdon, [June 1830] and June [1830], see below.

brief factory stint contrasts with the career of Louisa Sawyer, who worked in a number of mills in Lowell between the ages of thirteen and twenty-seven. When she married in 1853, at the age of thirty, she had been supporting herself for fully seventeen years. More typical of most women workers was Mary Paul. She left employment in domestic service and began work at the Lawrence Manufacturing Company in Lowell at the age of fifteen. She continued to work off and on in Lowell for four or four and a half years when she returned to live with her shoemaker father in Claremont, New Hampshire. She supported herself, though no longer in the mills, for the next seven years until she married Isaac Guild and settled in Lynn, Massachusetts. Mary Paul's four-year career in the mills was more typical than were the experiences of either Ann Blake or Louisa Sawyer.

Some interesting patterns emerge among the nine letter writers or their sisters who worked in textile mills. On average, the women began employment at sixteen and a half and continued to work for five and a half years, until just after reaching twenty-two. Furthermore, all nine did marry after their periods of mill employment. Finally, although they all married, their mean age at marriage, 27.5, was considerably higher than usual for women in this period. Nine cases, however, is a tiny population upon which to base any generalizations and we should broaden our data before placing much confidence in these numbers.

There is considerable evidence that the letter writers were rather typical of mill women in these years. About 80 percent of women residing in boardinghouses of the Hamilton Manufacturing Company in Lowell in 1830 and 1840 were between the ages of fifteen and twenty-nine, a proportion consistent with the ages at which the letter writers began and ended mill employment. For the group of 175 New Hampshire women I traced back from the Hamilton Company fully 85 percent began work before twenty-five. More than 90 percent remained unmarried when they completed their mill careers at Hamilton; and 85 percent of those who could be traced did marry. Finally, a contemporary observer, Henry Miles, collected statistics from mill agents and estimated in 1845 that the average length of time women had been employed in the mills was between four and five years.[50]

In terms of their ages at marriage, the letter writers also appear to have been quite representative. To place this evidence within a broader context, one may compare the marriage patterns of female millhands with those of nonmigrants from Boscawen, Canterbury, and Sutton, New

50. Dublin, *Women at Work*, pp. 31, 258; Miles, *Lowell As It Was*, p. 194.

Hampshire. First, millhand women tended to marry at a later age than did local women of this same generation who remained at home. The median age at marriage for millhands was 25.2, in contrast to a figure of 22.9 for nonmigrants. In addition, migrant women married men much closer to their own age than did nonmigrants. Husbands of millhands had a median age at marriage of 24.5 compared to 26.5 for husbands of nonmigrants.[51] Whereas millhands on the average were slightly older than their husbands, nonmigrant women were more than three and a half years younger. The difference here is striking.

That the marriage patterns of millhands should be viewed as unusual is confirmed if we consider other studies. All existing evidence on age at first marriage in nineteenth-century New England suggests that women typically married in their early twenties men who were several years older than themselves. Vital registration data for Massachusetts between 1845 and 1860, for instance, indicate that, on the average, men married 2.5 years later than did women. Vermont state figures for 1858 show men marrying at an average age of 24.6 years and women at 21.4. Local community studies confirm these findings. In Sturbridge, Massachusetts, between 1820 and 1849, women married for the first time at a mean age of 25.5; for men the comparable figure was 27.8. Finally, for the Massachusetts towns of Concord and Hingham, in roughly these years, men and women married at 26 and 23 years of age respectively. The dominant cultural pattern here is clear.[52]

The difference in the marriage patterns of millhands and nonmigrants probably stems from the fact that in the years before marriage mill women were separated from their families, living away from home and supporting themselves. It is likely that the economic and social independence that they achieved was reflected in their choice of spouse. Parents probably had only a limited voice in the final selection, especially for those who met their husbands while working away from home. And by virtue of having waited longer to marry, female millhands chose from a pool of men closer to their own age. The savings women brought with

51. These statistics are based on 80 married millhands and the 36 husbands for whom age at first marriage could be determined; for nonmigrants, the respective numbers are 168 women and 121 husbands.

52. Thomas Monahan, *The Pattern of Age at First Marriage in the United States* (Philadelphia: the author, 1951), pp. 161, 174-76, 316-18; Nancy Osterud and J. Fulton, "Family Limitation and Age at Marriage, 1730-1850," *Population Studies* (1976), 30:481-94; Marc Harris, "A Demographic Study of Concord, Massachusetts, 1750-1850" (Undergraduate honors thesis, Brandeis University, 1973), p. 42; Daniel Scott Smith, "Parental Power and Marriage Patterns: An Analysis of Historical Trends in Hingham, Massachusetts," *Journal of Marriage and the Family* (1973), 35:419-28.

them and the similarity of partners' ages may have placed the men and women in these marriages on a more equal footing than would have been the case for most rural couples. In all, data on age at marriage suggest that mill employment set women apart from others and prepared them for marriages that represented something of a departure from traditional patterns.[53]

Millhands and nonmigrants differed in another respect. Husbands of millhands were much less likely to be farmers than those of nonmigrants. Only a third of the husbands of millhands from Boscawen, Canterbury, or Sutton were farmers; among nonmigrants, in contrast, the proportion stood at more than 70 percent. Initially, one might argue that the difference simply reflected the fact that a large proportion of former millhands resided in cities and mill towns and were thus unlikely to take up farming. However, even if we restrict the comparison to couples who settled in rural areas, a substantial difference in husbands' occupations persists. Among these couples, only 42 percent of husbands of former millhands were farmers, compared to 73 percent of the husbands of nonmigrant women.[54] The mill experience, even when it lasted only a few years, had a permanent impact on women. Few followed entirely in their mothers' footsteps and became farmers' wives.

Millhands differed from nonmigrants in still another area of their married lives: childbearing. Judging from 1850 census listings former millhands had fewer children than nonmigrants. Controlling for age, and comparing women between the ages of thirty and thirty-nine, we find that former millhands had an average of 2.2 children living with them compared to 2.7 children for nonmigrants. So, it appears that millhands not only postponed marriage, but had fewer children than did women who remained in their rural hometowns.[55]

The women's letters and the evidence on marriage patterns suggest the changes that many women went through as they moved from farm to factory. The urban experience may have made them restless and unfit for the slower, more traditional life they had known; or, perhaps women who worked in the mills were particularly receptive to this new urban, industrial world. In any event, the letters of women workers and the writings of New Englanders critical of the movement into the mills pro-

53. For similar evidence for European working women in this period, see Tilly and Scott, *Women, Work, and Family,* p. 123.
54. These statistics are based on twenty-four husbands of former millhands and eighty-four husbands of nonmigrant women listed in the 1850 census.
55. This difference in fertility also holds if we control for the length of marriage for women in the two groups.

vide numerous indications that contemporaries were conscious of the tension between the two worlds and cultures—the urban world of the mill towns and the rural world of the surrounding countryside.

One New Hampshire historian, herself the sister of two Lowell operatives, captured an element of this tension in a brief description of the experience of going to the mills for women of her town:

> The girls began to go to work in the cotton factories of Nashua and Lowell. It was an all-day ride, but that was nothing to be dreaded. It gave them a chance to behold other towns and places, and see more of the world than most of the generation had ever been able to see. They went in their plain, country-made clothes, and after working several months, would come home for a visit, or perhaps to be married, in their tasteful city dresses, and with more money in their pockets than they had ever owned before.[56]

Augusta Worthen wrote these lines in 1890, looking back on the mill experience with an appropriate sense of distance. Other contemporaries, however, did not look so calmly upon their daughters returning with "tasteful city dresses, and more money . . . than they had ever owned before." Zadock Thompson, in an 1842 work, described much the same phenomenon in a more judgmental tone: "It is too common for farmers' daughters to grow up young ladies, play the piano . . . and spend their father's surplus funds for fine clothing."[57] Perhaps the women Thompson decried had picked up their tastes in mill towns or from sisters who worked there.

The problem was not simply that some rural observers watched their migrant daughters and found them wanting. Others felt that the judgment was mutual, that these young women rejected the values of their parents. An 1858 article made just this point:

> The most intelligent and enterprising of the farmer's daughters become school-teachers, or tenders of shops, or factory girls. They contemn the calling of their father, and will nine times out ten, marry a mechanic in preference to a farmer. They know that marrying a farmer is a serious business. They remember their worn-out mothers.[58]

The lines recall the marriage patterns of the women workers from the Hamilton Company. They were farmers' daughters, all right, but seven

---

56. *The History of Sutton, New Hampshire* (Concord, N.H.: Republican Press Association, 1890), p. 192.

57. *The History of Vermont, Natural, Civil, and Statistical, in Three Parts* (Burlington, Vt.: Chauncey Goodrich, 1842), p. 39.

58. *Atlantic Monthly* (Aug. 1858), p. 341.

times out of ten they married a mechanic "in preference to a farmer." They chose not to follow in the footsteps of their "worn-out mothers."

The last example is particularly pointed because it shifts the emphasis away from the reaction of others and focuses on the attitudes of women themselves. Passages in the letters of a number of mill women reveal that they did in fact make just these sorts of negative judgments about rural life. Maria and Lura Currier, two sisters from Wentworth, New Hampshire, worked in Lowell in the 1840s. In the winter of 1845-1846 they wrote to a friend and fellow operative in Lowell. Their parents would not allow them to go to Lowell that winter and they felt most discontented. As Lura wrote: "I cannot as you anticipated tell you of any pleasant sleigh rides . . . of the nice supper, and *turnovers* for they have no ambition for anything of that kind, up here in these *diggins*." Social life in Wentworth seemed barren indeed after all the excitement and bustle of city life: "It is extremely dull here now, there is nothing at all interesting going on here, save the orthodox have a singing school, but *that, we* do not attend." To the Currier sisters all the lively and interesting people seemed to be going to the mill towns. Wrote Maria: "A great many of our young people are leaving this Spring for Manchester and Lowell." It was a long winter and spring for the two sisters who had their hearts set on returning to Lowell.[59]

Mary Paul also developed a degree of sophistication that led her to look down upon certain aspects of rural life and culture. Several years after she left Lowell, she moved to a utopian cooperative community in New Jersey. While working there she was surprised to meet a couple from her hometown in Vermont, who were on something of a sightseeing tour that included this community. As Mary wrote to her father: "They are travelling for pleasure I expect and came here to *see* as people go to Niagara [Falls] to see." Mary expressed the distance between herself and her visitors when she noted: "They are real nice folks but seem rather countryfied in their ideas."[60]

The complaints of Zadock Thompson and the comments of the Currier sisters and Mary Paul provide contrasting views of the same basic dilemma. Women workers in the early mills were caught between two worlds. Born and raised in rural New England, they identified with the pride and independence of their yeoman farmer parents. At the same time, however, they experienced a new life and enjoyed the social and

59. Lura Currier to Harriet Hanson, Dec. 14, 1845; Maria Currier to Harriet Hanson, April 5, 1846, Harriet Hanson Robinson Collection, Schlesinger Library, Radcliffe College.
60. Mary Paul to Bela Paul, June 11, 1855, see below.

economic independence it provided. They returned home with new clothes and with periodicals and more modern ideas picked up in the fluid urban setting. They also came back with money in their pockets and spending habits that surprised some of their rural neighbors. For many, work in the mills proved to be a first and irreversible step away from the rural, agricultural lives of their parents. A good proportion found the life of the mill town too alluring to return to rural villages. Even those who went back home tended to marry nonfarmers and thus did not follow in the footsteps of their mothers. For both groups, those who remained in the country and those who settled in cities, the mill experience signaled the beginning of a new life. Through the letters of Sarah Hodgdon, Louisa Sawyer, Persis Edwards, Mary Paul, and Delia Page we can begin to appreciate the personal meaning of this broader phenomenon.

Note on the Editing of the Letters

In editing the letters and accounts presented in this collection I have tried to preserve the character of the originals. I have adhered to the following practices in transcribing and editing:

1. Spelling is preserved as found in the original. Only where errors obscure the meaning have I used the admonitory [sic]. Occasionally I have spelled what I take to be the word intended within square brackets.

2. Grammar and syntax are preserved as found in the original.

3. Capitalization and punctuation are unchanged except that sentences begin with a capital letter and end with a period. Where periods were lacking, they have been silently added. Dashes at the end of a sentence have been changed to periods. Any punctuation marks added to clarify meaning are enclosed in square brackets.

4. Any letters or words supplied to make a passage intelligible are enclosed in square brackets.

5. Two letters written on the same sheet of paper or enclosed within the same envelope are divided by a single hairline rule. Separate letters are otherwise divided by a double hairline rule.

View of Lowell, 1830, as Sarah Hodgdon would have seen it.

ONE

The Hodgdon Letters

SARAH AND ELIZABETH HODGDON were the eldest children of Abner and Mary Hodgdon of Rochester, New Hampshire. Abner Hodgdon was an established, prosperous member of the community. He was a trustee of the Methodist Church. By 1850 he worked seventy-five acres of improved land, a substantial holding valued at $2000.[1] While his two sons may have worked alongside him, his daughters left home in their mid-teens to find paid employment. Sarah departed in 1830 to take up work in a textile factory; two years later Elizabeth began teaching school. She found her first position in her hometown, but soon shifted to more distant districts. The two sisters kept up a healthy correspondence with their family, a fact that permits us to compare their experiences in two of the most important occupations for women before the Civil War.[2]

The first letters in the collection trace Sarah's mill experience in Lowell and in Great Falls, New Hampshire between 1830 and 1840. Sarah began work at the Merrimack Company in Lowell at the age of sixteen. She went there with a friend, Elizabeth, probably not her sister, and an older neighbor, Wealthy Page, who had evidently worked in Lowell previously. The three resided together in a company boardinghouse and worked in the same weaving room. Several of Wealthy's letters have survived, and they indicate the supportive role she played with the mill newcomers. As she wrote, probably to the Hodgdon family: "I am the same friend to Sarah that I was when I promised to befriend her."[3]

1. Franklin McDuffee, *History of the Town of Rochester, New Hampshire, From 1722 to 1890,* 2 vols. (Manchester, N.H.: John B. Clarke, 1892), 1:265; 1850 Manuscript Census of Agriculture for Rochester.
2. The mill letters of Sarah Hodgdon and Wealthy Page are included in the Hodgdon Family Letters, New Hampshire Historical Society, while those Elizabeth wrote while teaching are found in the Sanborn Family Papers, Massachusetts Historical Society (hereafter cited as MHS).
3. Family Record, Sanborn Family Papers, MHS; Wealthy Page to "Dear friends," [June, 1830] below. The Hodgdon and Page families lived two houses apart according to the 1830 Census of Rochester.

Sarah Hodgdon needed Wealthy's support and guidance. Although she was a member of the Freewill Baptist Church in Rochester, Sarah received a cool reception from fellow parishioners in Lowell. Her problems were twofold: first, she did not feel she could afford to pay the "pew rent" customary in urban churches at this date; second, she attended the Methodist Meeting with Wealthy, an event which did not go unnoticed by acquaintances of the Freewill Baptist denomination. Sarah wrote home seeking parental support and advice. Initially she asked for help in "hiring a seat" so that she could attend regularly. After being snubbed at later services, however, she asked her mother "to write me what to do wether it is best to go to the babptist or to the methodist." The outcome of her dilemma is unknown, but that it proved a wrenching experience for Sarah cannot be doubted.

This incident raises a theme that is recurrent in the correspondence of mill women in this period. It is clear that Sarah Hodgdon, although separated from her family, was by no means estranged or emotionally distant. Consider the line near the end of her first letter home: "Give my love to my farther tell him not to forget me and to my dear sister and to my brothers and to my grammother tell her I do not forget her and to my Aunts and to all my enquiring friends." Another letter ends with a poem expressing her homesickness: "I want to se[e] you more I think/Than I can write with pen and ink."

The continuing bond with family is evident in the ways Sarah sought advice from her parents. She first asked advice about her church difficulties. Later, while working in the mills in Great Falls, she asked her mother and sister if they thought she should come home. Her sister responded, "we do not know better than you or so well either when you have earned as much as you will want to spend." The strength of the familial bond was such that although she had been working away from home off and on for almost ten years, she still felt a need for parental advice.

Elizabeth Hodgdon's response reflects an important element in the lives of women in the early mills—their newfound economic independence. These letters underscore the economic and social independence that Yankee mill women enjoyed in the years between 1830 and 1850. Rarely did families migrate to mill towns with their daughters. From letters it is clear that women's earnings were their own, to spend as wisely or as foolishly as they chose. In some cases sheer economic necessity may have led women to enter the mills and to save every spare cent of their wages to assist their families. Most mill women came, however, from propertied farming families and absolute deprivation was not a strong motivating factor. For demographic reasons—i.e., too many children for too little land—the women's prospects of settling in their home-towns on comfortable farms may have been slim. Thus it made sense for them to keep an eye open to alternatives, but it is important to view mill employment as the choice that it was rather than as a necessity.

Sarah's mill career extended for at least ten years as she worked first at the Merrimack Company in Lowell and later at the Great Falls Manufacturing Company, only a few miles from her family home in Rochester. Elizabeth had a parallel career as a school teacher, working for at least eleven years, and the second half of this section focuses on her work experience. Numerous letters have survived from her teaching years, two of which are included here. In addition, she kept accounts (also reprinted below) of her earnings and expenses during her periods of employment in her hometown of Rochester, then in South Berwick, Maine, and finally in Great Falls. According to her accounts, she earned $185 between 1832 and 1841, a substantial figure since it probably represents her earnings above and beyond the cost of room and board.[4]

Women's employment in the antebellum years, whether in the common schools or textile mills, was generally restricted to the years before marriage and, for native-born women at least, there is little evidence of paid employment outside of the home by married women. And the work clearly did not in any way "unfit" women for marriage. Sarah and Elizabeth Hodgdon were quite typical in this respect. After mill work in Lowell and Great Falls, Sarah married William Jenness, a Rochester shoemaker, in December 1845. They continued to reside in Rochester, at least until 1860, although they do not appear to have had any children. After eleven years of teaching, Elizabeth married Nathan Colman, a seaman from Scituate, Massachusetts. The couple had one child, born in August 1850, but parents and child died within three weeks of each other before the end of the year.[5]

Such was the place of the work experience of the Hodgdon sisters in the perspective of their broader lives. We know little about the years before and after these letters, but for this period at least we get a glimpse into their daily activities and concerns. And, although Sarah Hodgdon requested that her mother "not let this scrabbling be seen," we can hope she would forgive our intrusion into this otherwise private world.

4. See Elizabeth's letters, school certificates, and accounts in Sanborn Family Papers, MHS. Great Falls was the mill district within the larger town of Somersworth.
5. Family Record, Sanborn Family Papers, MHS; New Hampshire Bureau of Vital Records, marriage records; 1850 Census of Rochester, dwelling 2423, 1860 Census of Rochester, dwelling 386, 1850 Census of Somersworth, dwelling 329. See also Elizabeth Hodgdon to Nathan Colman, Sept. 8, 1844, Sanborn Family Papers, MHS.

Letters of Sarah Hodgdon and Wealthy Page, 1830

[June 1830]

Dear mother

I take this opertunity to write to you to informe you that I have gone into the mill and like very well. I was here one week and three days before I went into the mill to work for my board. We boord t[o]gether. I like my boording place very well. I enjoy my health very well. I do not enjoy my mind so well as it is my desire to. I cant go to any meetings except I hire a seat therefore I have to stay home on that acount.[6] I desire you pay that it may not be said of me when I come home that I have sold my soul for the gay vanitys of this world. Give my love to my farther tell him not to forget me and to my dear sister and to my brothers and to my grammother tell her I do not forget her and to my Aunts and to all my enquiring friends.[7] I want that you should write to me as soon as you can and when you write to me I want that you should write to me the particulars about sister and Aunt Betsy. Dont fail writing. I bege you not to let this scrabling be seen.

Sarah Hodgdon

Mary Hodgdon

Lowell June 6 1830

Respected friends

Feeling anxious to see you and more so to hear from you I resume my pen for the purpose of writing you a few imperfect lines. In Sarahs letter Sarah and Elizabeth appear to be very well contented like better than they expected. Sarah has been tending Looms alone. Elizabeth and I are tending four.[8] Sarahs health is very good and she has been very steady since she has been here. We all board together. Sarah is rather

6. Sarah's reference here is to the quarterly "pew rent" common in urban churches in this period.

7. From the Family Record we can reconstruct the Hodgdon family. The parents were Abner and Mary, forty-five and forty-two years old respectively at this date. In addition to Sarah and Elizabeth, sixteen and fourteen years old, children included George, eleven, and John, seven, at the time of this letter.

8. Wealthy Page describes an unusual practice here. Normally each weaver tended two looms at this date. It appears that Wealthy and Elizabeth were assigned a double complement of four looms and worked together. Women often assisted one another from time to time in the course of the working day, but Wealthy and Elizabeth seem to have formalized this pattern.

unwilling to go to meeting on account of hiring a seat. I want you should write what you think about it. I wrote to brother Benjamin the week after I left and have been to the post office a number of times to receive an answer and felt quite disappointed.[9] Tell them that I should be glad for them to write. Give my love to all that ask for me and accept a double share to your self. Do write soon. Elizabeth sends love to you all and to Mrs York and family likewise. She says that you and Mrs York seem more like a mother than any one else.[10] Excuse my scrabling. We arrived here safe monday about five o'clock had a very pleasant ride. The times are not quite so good as they were when I left here but are growing better. I hope we shall be favoured with health which is the greatest blessing we can enjoy. When you feel to pour out your soul to God and direct your prayers to the throne of mercy then dont forget us who are far distant from you. When I think of home and the sufferings of my dear Brother it oft causes a heaving sigh and a falling tear and then I retire and breathe a prayer to Almi[ghty] Father in Heaven that he would protect me from sin and danger and from the vain things of this flattering world and fit and prepare [me] for heaven and imortal glory and there to praise him to one eternal day and there methinks if I continue to pray and faint not and hold out to the end watch and be sober do the commands of God I hope one day to meet you all with my Dear Brother to part no more is the sincere prayer and desire of your unworthy friend.

Wealthy Page

Give our best love to Father. Tell him we dont forget him. Don't let this be seen.

Lowell June [1830]

Dear Sister and mother

I resume my pen to write to you to informe the perticulars as you requested to know. As it respects my health it is very good and I am

9. Wealthy's brother and father were both named Benjamin. According to the 1830 Census Benjamin Page, who was between sixty and seventy years old, resided two houses away from the Hodgdons. Ten years later, another Benjamin Page, this one forty to fifty years old and probably Wealthy's brother, lived near the Hodgdons with no household members old enough to be his parents.

10. Mrs. York may have been a neighbor of the Hodgdons and the Pages. The 1830 manuscript census of Rochester records a John York and his family residing next door to the Pages and three houses away from the Hodgdons. The reference to Elizabeth here makes it clear that she is not a Hodgdon, but rather a close friend of the family.

very well conte[nte]d as to my work but a very diagreeable
circumstance has taken place which gives me many gloomy hours. By
the devine aid of God I will endeavor to relate to you a few perticulars.
When I first come to this place when I had been here a few hours I
was introdused to a young lady belonging to the freewillbabptist
connection. She asked me if belonged to the freewillbabtist. I told I did
[and] she invited me to go to meeting. I went had a very good meeting
and in a few days she grew cold and indifferent towards me. A few
days previous to this Wealthy invited me to go to meeting with her.
Agreeable to her request I went. I [e]njoied myself very well. Do no let
these things trouble you for by the goodness of God I trust that I shall
get throug[h] at last and enjoy your society. I have one good friend
here in lowell that is a mother to me as it were. It is my prayer to God
that he would reward her for all that love and affections that she has
shone towards me. I know when I was in Rochester that the brethren
seemed to fellowship me so much as think they had ough[t] to for one
that belongs to there connection. I think that it is on the account of that
girle that I menthioned in the former part of my letter. I have not done
nor said any thing to caus this girle to say any thing about me an[d]
W[ealthy] knows for she has been with me every where I have been
and she says any time that I want to go out that she will go with me.
Many things more might be menth[i]oned but time will not permit.

[Sarah]

Don't let this be seen.

Dear Farther[11]

   We gladly recieved a letter (or not worthy to be called a letter it was
so small) from Elisabeth and likewise from Benjamin and mother. I
was ple[a]s[ed] to here that you was well and get along so well in your
business. When you write again I want you write a whole letter. If you
cant find words enough to fill a sheet of paper get some of your
neighbors to healp you. As you have given your concent beloved father
fore me to come to this place I hope that you will have no cause to be
sory. I want you to write to me as soon as you can afoard time to.

[Sarah]

Dont let this be seen.

11. The next two letters appear on the same sheets as the previous one and
though undated were probably written at the same time.

Dearly beloved mother

I do not want this letter to trouble you that I wrote to you but I want you to write to me what to do wether it is best to go to the babptist or to the methodist.[12] I feel well contented much better than I thoug[ht] that i should. Give my love to all my friends. Tell littel johnny that I have got his juiceharp and tell georgegy that I will bring him home something when I come home.[13]

yours &c

Sarah H

To my deare father an mother an sister and all the rest.

> I want to se[e] you more I think
> Than I can write with pen an ink
> But when I shall I canot tell
> But from my heart I wish you well
> I wish you well from all my heart
> Although we are so far apart
> if you die there and I die here
> before one God we shall apeare.[14]

[June 1830]

Dear friends

Let me assure you that I am just the same friend to Sarah that I was when I promised to befriend her. It has grieved me very much to see the coldness which she has been treatd with since we have been here by [them] that call themselves free will Baptist.[15] I think they are as they might be calld self will and rightly namd. I go to the Methodist and have offerd to find Sarah and Elizabeth both a seat there if they will go with me. They thought they should like to go to their own meeting but since they have been talkd so hard to for not hiring a seat and [not] going to ther meeting all their time they have almost concluded to go with me. Sarah nor Elizabeth has give them no

12. By 1830 all the Hodgdons seem to have been members in the Freewill Baptist Church in Rochester. They had been members of the Methodist Church earlier, however.

13. The "juiceharp" referred to here was undoubtedly a Jew's harp, a small musical instrument held in the mouth and played by striking or plucking with the hands.

14. This poem does not appear to be original. For a subsequent use, see *The Lowell Offering* (1841), 1:245.

15. The Freewill Baptist Church in Rochester was founded during a revival in 1829, with Sarah Hodgdon listed as an original member. McDuffee, *History of Rochester*, 1:278.

occasion to treat them so coldly. Sarah felt as if she wanted you to
know it. You must let no one see this. Dont let what we have wrote
trouble you any. Sarah is well and appears to be contented. She has
had a Dollar a week ever since she has been in the Mill. Her overseer
told her that she might tend looms alone and all she could earn over a
Dollar she might have but shoud have a dollar a week at any rate.[16]

I hope you will keep this letter a secret and write soon.

Wealthy Page

Sarah has bought her a very handsome Scotch gingham two shillings
pr yard.[17]

Lowell July 12 1830

Good morning. B and H[18]

How is your health this morning? I hope this scroll will find you as
well as it leaves the writer. We received your letter and was very glad.
Elizabeth wants to see you all very much. I hope you will excuse my
scrabling this morning for I have been taking down some of the heads
of my lesson. I go to the Bible class and I allmost think they give me a
very hard lesson. Mr. Avery the Methodist preacher is the teacher of
our class and he questions us very closely.[19] I should like to had
E[lizabeth] gone with me but she thought she could not get her lesson.
We began at the first of Genesis and are going through the old and
new testament. Our first lesson was five chapters and the next was six.
I have to study I tell you. I suppose you have heard enough about this
subject so I will pass on. Mr Ball gave Elizabeth looms by the side of

16. Wealthy is quoting Sarah's earnings above board. The weekly cost of
room and board in company boardinghouses came to $1.25 at this date,
making Sarah's overall earnings $2.25 per week. Since Sarah was not tending
looms alone at this time, she must have been a "sparehand," an operative
assigned to assist a more experienced worker while she learned the basic
skills of weaving. At the Hamilton Company in Lowell in July 1836, spare-
hands earned on the average $0.44 per day, while regular weavers earned
$0.66. For further discussion see Thomas Dublin, *Women at Work: The Trans-
formation of Work and Community in Lowell, Massachusetts, 1826-1860* (New
York: Columbia University Press, 1979), ch. 4.

17. It was quite common in Lowell to quote wages and prices in English
currency. With six shillings equivalent to a dollar, Sarah's Scotch gingham
cost $0.33 per yard.

18. These are Benjamin, Wealthy's brother, and his wife, Huldah. 1850 Census of Rochester, dwelling 2301.

19. Mr. Avery here is Edward K. Avery, pastor of the First Methodist Church
in Lowell.

me so I can help her when I am not tending four myself.[20] You said something in your letter about Sister A wanting to know where I was. I should like for you to write me what she said after she heard where I had gone. I should like to know what she said about it. I have felt rather sorry that I did not go up there whether they wanted me to or not. I think if I were to come home again that nothing would prevent me from going to see her. You must tell her she must write and Mr. chesley too. I have felt sorry for one person that I did not see when I was at home. A funny kind of a letter you will say I have wrote here. It is what has popd into my head this morning and I have wrote just as fast as I thought. You will conclude so by the scrabling. It has got to be almost meeting time and I must close my narrative hoping you will let no one see it but burn it immediately. I want you should write me a long letter as quick as possible. If any one should come here from your way that you know of tell them if they will call at Mr C Brown No. 45 or at the Merrimic incorporation counting room. I shoud be pleasd to see any one that come from that way.[21] Where I board is where I told you. I come to see those twin children Matthew and Mary. They often remind me of Elizabeth and Olive. How glad should I be to see them and little William too. Kiss them all for me.

Wealthy Page

I hope you will let no one see this. I have been reading it over and am good mind not to send it. I would not but I trust to your honesty you will let no one see it for conscience sake. Tell Mrs Hodgdon Sarah is well. Give our love to father. I think I shall write to him soon. Tell Miss M Foss if you see her I have not ascertaind any news concerning her beau. I have made inquiry but no one knew any thing about him. I guess this is not the Billericca where he belongs.[22]

---

20. The 1832 Lowell *Directory* recorded an Abner Ball, manufacturer, living at 23 Dutton Street. This was one of the tenements owned by the Merrimack Company, and Ball is probably the overseer Wealthy mentions here. The reference to four looms is unclear. In the 1830s weavers normally tended only two looms; perhaps Wealthy was required at times to assume the work of an absent weaver.

21. Wealthy, Elizabeth, and Sarah Hodgdon appear to have worked at the Merrimack Company and lived in a boardinghouse kept by Charles Brown. Brown resided at 45 Worthen Street and worked as an overseer in the Merrimack dye house according to the 1832 Lowell *Directory*. The "counting room" mentioned here would have been the business office of the mill. Whenever a visitor hoped to see a friend during the working day, he or she would have to inquire first at the counting room.

22. Billerica is the next town just south of Lowell.

Merrimack Company, Lowell, Massachusetts, c. 1830.

Letters of John and Elizabeth Hodgdon, 1840

Rochester March the 29 1840

Dear sister,[23]

I take this time to write you a few lines as I have a good opportunity. I thank you for your letter you sent sister and myself; and I find you have not forgotten me (your unworthy Brother). As you wrote to me about never working there again I hope you will never be under the necesity of it but I hope you will not put to[o] much dependence on your absent fri[e]nd for you know not neather do any of us what time will bring forth but God alone knows and if we put our trust in him he will bring all things for the best.[24] Therefore let us look to him alone and he will brings things out right. You said if I mistake not you have not seen a well day since your absence. I am sory to hear that for it pained me to the hart and brought me to reflect on myself when sick from home. But it was not so hard for me having a sister to comfort me in my illness. I supose sister that I shall come after you if nothing particular prevents me. So you can give your notice when you please and send us word and we will move you home as you say.

Yours with respect Sarah D Hodgdon

Your most affectionate brother John B. Hodgdon

I have forgoten one thing; Mr Hays Lydias farther Layes at the point of Deth. He has a feaver and has been sick about or little over a week. His fri[e]nds have given him up and the Doctor says it is a doutful case.

[Rochester, March 29, 1840]

Dear Sister

Do not think I have forgotten you because I have not written for there has always been something to prevent me so that I could not write & the alarm concerning the small pet entirely ceased soon after you went away & I thought you would probably hear of it therefore I did not feel so anxious about writing as if it had been otherwise.

23. John Hodgdon, age seventeen, is addressing his sister Sarah, employed in the mills of nearby Great Falls, N.H.

24. The identity of the "absent friend" mentioned here is uncertain, but there can be no doubt that John Hodgdon is referring to a possible marriage. The person may have been a cousin, John Brewster. Elizabeth writes to Sarah about Brewster in the letter dated Oct. — 1841 below. Brewster died at sea and Sarah later married William Jenness, a shoemaker in Rochester.

Sister Sarah I suppose you feel by this time as though you had worked long enough in the factory & I should think the money you wrote me you had erned with what you had before would be as much as you would need to spend during this year, you know. The patterns you sent me I do not like very much. Respecting Florence bonnets I think they are to[o] costly for us & in fact they last too long; but if you think you should prefer them I have not a word to say. I think it will not be possible for me to go down while you work there so if you make any purchases I have only to say satisfy yourself & I assure you I shall not be dissatisfied. Study what will be profitable & becoming for us the ensuing season if we should live to enjoy it which may it be the pleasure & will of Divine Providence that we may & be blest in fully realizing what our fond hopes now anticipate.

You say you want to come home when we all think you have staid long enough but we do not know better than you or so well either when you have earned as much as you will want to spend. Yet it is Mothers opinion & mine that you have already as much as you will probably want to spend if you lay it out to good advantage which we doubt not but you will. We want you to make arrangements to suit yourself to give your notice as soon as you please & settle all up & send us word so that we may know when to send for you or move you home as you say.

All are well in this place excepting Mr Hayes of whom John has wrote. It is really a distressed house & an affecting scene to see relatives weeping over him. All the children are at home excepting Ichabod whom they expect next Wednesday. Moses was over here last Friday after Aunt Liberty to go & take care of him but she could not go.[25] He said he wished you was at home that he might get you to go & said something about going down after you. But I should advise you not to go if he did but dont you let him know that I said any thing against it. Yet I think on the whole that he will not go for you now the doing is so bad and the house is already quite full.

Be sure to send us word as soon as you learn how your time is limited. Give my love to Lucy & accept much to yourself.[26]

From your affectionate sister
Elizabeth K. Hodgdon

Sarah D. Hodgdon
Rochester March 29th 1840

25. Aunt Liberty was a younger sister of Abner Hodgdon. Family Record, Sanborn Family Papers, MHS.
26. The identity of Lucy is unclear, but she was probably a mutual Rochester friend who accompanied Sarah to work in Great Falls.

Great Falls Manufacturing Company, c. 1840.

Letters and Accounts of Elizabeth Hodgdon, 1840-1841

[Great Falls, N.H. July 24 —][27]

Dear Parents

Supposing you feel solicitous to know respecting the closing up of my school & when I shall be ready to return home I will just inform you that my school will close tomorrow & I shall be ready to go home on Saturday afternoon. Yet if it is not convenient for you to send for me then Monday will suit me as well. I should like for Sarah to come down if it is convenient. If not send any one you please. I saw Mr Brusbridge yesterday.[28] He said they should expect me to teach next term. We shall [have] 2 weeks vacation which will give us an opportunity to rest you know. And I really feel as though I needed to rest (my patience if nothing more) for a little while & then I shall feel as though I could commence again with new courage. Every day has brought such a continual round of duties & every night brought me to such a peaceful home that the time has glided away in a manner almost insensibly to me. It seems to me that it cannot have been three months since I have been here. I suppose now is what we call right in the heighth of haying & I feel as though I should enjoy a ramble in the fields & pastures very much as it would bring to mind the fond recollection of past times. And I am (as you have often expressed about yourself Mother!) in my night reveries always at home in some sequestered spot in the field or busily engaged in domestic affairs for which you know I have some little relish & take some little pride in doing some little things. Now I doubt not but you will laugh at the folly of this letter but I must beg you will excuse it for I have written in such a hurry I hardly know what I have said. Now it is almost school time & I will defer the rest of the news till I get home.

One thing more however. Mrs Chandler is going east next week & wants her Mother to come down & take care of Mary while she is gone for she says she never can take the trouble to carry her. And if she cannot come down here she wants her to take her up there. And if she can do neither she wants me to take her home with me & says I shall be well paid for it. I want you to find out and let her know when you come down. But I do not want to take her home even if Mrs Furber cannot take of her unless you, Father & Mother, feel perfectly willing.

[Elizabeth]

---

27. The letter has no heading but place and date are taken from the postmark on the envelope. The year is probably 1840 or 1841.
28. G.W. Brusbridge appears to have been a member of the Prudential

Friday evening Oct — 1841

Dear Sister[29]

When I returned from school this evening supper was on the table & the family already partaking of the evening repast. As I entered the room said Mrs Chandler[30] there is something for you in the clock-case from Rochester. What is it? But no sooner was the question asked than your letter in my hands answered it. Its contents were of course perused before I took *my* seat at the table & as soon as natures demands were satisfied I took my light & the letter & retired to the parlour. Having reread your letter I again take up my pen to say a few words to you. I have written & sealed a letter for you this morning but as you seemed to think *one* would be so joyfully received I thought two would increase the pleasure in a twofold proportion so I seated myself before the table & here I have written a long introduction not knowing half what I have said for I have penned thoughts just as they came into my head without any quallification whatever as you have already probably judged. But however just between you & I it is no matter you know. Well, after school I went into Miss Youngs shop to see about my bonnet. I looked over all her new bonnet silks & velvets. Some of them I like very much but I think on the whole the velvet preferable to any thing else for a winter bonnet. I inquired the price of the various pieces & find that I cannot get any thing for a decent bonnet to wear in this place for less than four dollars. But I shall not have mine made till I hear from you again which I shall expect to by D. Ricker when he returns from Rochester.

I have not seen Rosettas letter since a week ago last Wednesday but I can tell you all there was in it. She spoke of his safe arrival in Boston in the afternoon of the day he left here & also that the ship Surat had not arrived.[31] Then he mentioned the request of the merchants for him

School Committee of Great Falls. In a letter dated April 24, 1840, he offered Elizabeth a teaching position at a salary of $12 per month. Sanborn Family Papers, MHS.

29. This letter is addressed to Sarah Hodgdon back in Rochester. Elizabeth is apparently nearing the end of another term of teaching in Great Falls and will soon be returning home.

30. Judging from context it would appear that Elizabeth is boarding in the Chandler household while teaching school.

31. The identity of Rosetta is uncertain, but the man referred to here is John Brewster, probably a cousin of Sarah and Elizabeth. Brewster was a sailor and, as Elizabeth indicates below, perhaps a captain. He was also a shipmate of Nathan J. Colman who married Elizabeth in 1844. He may have been engaged to Sarah Hodgdon, but he died at sea when he was knocked overboard in a storm. See a condolence letter Elizabeth wrote Sarah, April 21, 1842; see also E.K. Brewster to Sarah Hodgdon, April 17, 1842, and Elizabeth Hodgdon to Nathan J. Colman, Oct. 31, 1841, Sanborn Family Papers, MHS.

to take the present voyage & said he I have made up my mind to go
but did not say a word about him having the command of the vessel.
He told Rosetta to tell Sarah that he delivered her letter to Mr Cooper
& that he liked the gentlemans appearance very much. He wished to be
remembered to all enquiring friends & subscribed himself her
affectionate Brother John Brewster. He spoke of Joshuas family that
they were all well & would have been very happy to have seen her in
Boston with J. You said in your letter that you had one written for J.
(I hope you have a copy of it.) Respecting the backing of the letter I
will subjoin the following as a specimen of what I should think would
be correct & then you can do as you please.
Mr John Brewster
    Alexandria, Dis. of Columbia
      U.S.A.
As for the title of Capt you will do as you think proper about that. I
did not think of it when I commenced the signature so good night sis
for my hands are very cold & I must go down & warm them.

                              Saturdy morning
    His voyage I hope will be both safe & prosperous & as his ship
ploughs deeply through the waves glides steadily amidst the calm & at
lenght [sic] outrides the storms heaving in due time to the land of his
Father where his kindred spirits dwell. So may he after having goon
deep in search of pleasure serenely enjoy lifes blessings & when its
voyage is ended be safely landed where he will enjoy an eternity of
rest in the portals of peace in the kingdom of his Father.
    How soon will two weeks have passed away & I return (if life is
spared) to my home to enjoy another two weeks rest. This term has
already seemed to me very long I know not why & there are yet two
weeks not passed. But these will be weeks of much care & anxiety as a
review of all the lessons must be attended to in order to be prepared
for an examination. You may imagine what my feelings are as a
teacher but you cannot know them. They are different from those
resulting from any other occupation. In the school room we form a
little republic of which I am President. My subjects are not those with
whom I can concil & advise but I must hold the supreme sway over the
whole & not merely over my *room* to see that it is kept in order &
every thing aranged so as to preserve good order & prosperity but over
the human mind yes over the mind just unfolding in all its innocence
& loveliness—human depravity not out of the question—but there I
could write all day & not find where to stop. It is now school time & I
must leave you by bidding you all good morning.
                                    E. K. Hodgdon

Sister I want you to send me that old pen knife for I have lost the other & if you will have that sharpened & send it by D Ricker I shall be very much obliged. Dont fail to send it for I must have one Mondy at all events.

Tell John to be sure and bring those cat tail flays the next time he comes down. Mrs. C. wants them to give little Charles the tops & roots. Mother will know to tell him how much. Brother John be sure & write so as to send by D.R.

[Elizabeth Hodgdon's accounting of her earnings][32]

		$ cts.
1832	taught school in Rochester	
	11 weeks at $1. per week	11.
1836	taught school in Rochester	
	8 weeks at 10 1/2 shillings per week	14.
1837	taught school in Rochester 26 weeks	
	at 8 shillings per week	34.66 2/3
1838	4 days work at Mr Jenkings at 1/6[33] per day	1.
1839	2 ---- ---- -- -- --------- -- ---[34]	.30
	taught school in South Berwick	
	7 weeks at 2 2/7 dollars per week	16.
	made one pair of pantaloons at 3/ per pair	.50
1840	taught school in Somersworth 7 3/4 months	
	at 7 dollars per month[35]	54.25
1841	taught school in Somersworth 6 months	
	at 9 dollars per month	54.
	[Total Earnings over Period	185.72][36]

---

32. This accounting appears as an unlabeled sheet in Elizabeth Hodgdon's handwriting in the Sanborn Family Papers, MHS. There are minor arithmetic errors in the two accounts that I have left uncorrected.

33. Elizabeth is recording her daily wage here as one shilling, sixpence, or $0.25.

34. Dashes in this and the next account were used by Elizabeth Hodgdon as ditto marks.

35. The wage figure here, $7 per month, probably refers only to Elizabeth's earnings above her room and board. Her overall salary was most likely $12 per month.

36. Elizabeth did not total either this account or the next. I have summed the figures and rounded off to the nearest cent. Elizabeth's account covers the period 1832-1841, but she saved a number of receipts that indicate she kept teaching through the summer of 1843, earning at least another $78 after the closing of this account.

[Elizabeth Hodgdon's accounting of her expenditures]

1832	paid to Mrs Prickey 6 dollars for board & medicine	6.	
--33	---- Joshua Berry 2.50 for S[arah] and myself		
	attending writing schooll	2.50	
	bought 8 yds of calico at .14 per yd	1.12	
	------ 1 silk bonnet for 1.38	1.38	
--36	paid to Miss C. Knight for attending school	3.	
	---- for Geography & Atlas	1.	
	---- to Mr Ingalls for attending school	6.	
	---- for an Algebra	1.	
	---- --- -- Astronomy	.50	
	bought 1 new silk handkerchief for 1.	1.	
	2 combs at .28 per comb	.56	
	1 luce cape & with pink lining for .94	.94	
--37	2 lamps for .75	.75	
	2 vegetable dishes at .87 1/2 per dish	1.75	
	1 salt stand at 1/6	.25	
	4 yds of ribbon at 1/ per yard	.66	
	2 shawls at 6. per shawl	12.	
	3 1/2 yds white cambrick for 1.25	1.25	
	2 pair of gloves at .50 per pair	1.	
	1 ---- -- shoes at 6/ --- ----	1.	
	1 bunch of braid at 1/ per bunch	.16	2/3
	1 yd brown cambric at 1/ per yd	.16	2/3
	- -- white ------ edgeing at 1/--	.16	2/3
	1 spool of thread at .05 per spool	.05	
	paid to Aunt Sally 10.$ borrowed money	10.	
	bought 1 book Guide to Young Disciples for .37 cts	.37	
	12 yds unbleached cotton cloth at .15 per yd	1.80	
	3/4 yd of silk for work pockets &		
	pink braid for string	.50	
	2 1/2 yds of black velvet at 1.66 2/3	1.66	2/3
1839	bought 1 spool of thread at .05		
	5 skeins of thread at .03	.08	
	------ 3 sheets of paper for .03 6 quills for .06	.09	
	------ 1 skein of sewing silk for .04		
	1/2 yd black velvet for .25	.29	
	------ 1 varigated straw bonnet for 1.50	1.50	
	------ 1 pair of shoes for 1.12 1/2	1.12	1/2
	paid for mending shoes .18 for letter .06	.24	

bought wafers & pencil f[?] .02
        six yds ribbon for 1.68   1.72
     1 yd white linen .92
        3 yds unbleached linen for .90   1.82
     -- cotton cloth for .10 buttons for .04   .14
     1 broadcloth cap for 1. &
        1 pair of gloves for .50   1.50
     1 French Grammar -- .75 hair oil for .25 1.
     2 yds blue bind[in]g at .09
        slate & lead pencils at .03   .12
        soap [?] for .04 braid for .05   .09
paid Miss Haskell 3. for attending school 3.
     Mrs Hodgdon 4. --- board   4.

[Total Expenditures over Period   75.76]

Sabrina Bennett and her extended kinship network.

John Edwards
b. 1764
d. 1849

—m. 1784—

Betsy Holden
b. 1767
d. 1855

Betsey Edwards
b. 1786
m. Timothy Frisbee
- John L. Frisbee
- Rachel Frisbee

Hepzibah Edwards
b. 1788
m. Jeremiah Sawyer

John Sawyer, 1812	m. Phebe Ann Fields, 1838
Jeremiah Sawyer, 1814	d. in Lowell, 1840
Hepzibah Sawyer, 1816	m. John Buzzell, 1840
*Olive Sawyer, 1820	m. Simeon Brown, 1838
*Louisa Sawyer, 1823	m. Daniel Swan, 1852
Emeline Sawyer, 1826	m. Charles Geer, 1852
Daniel Sawyer, 1828	m. Julia Gibbons, 1851

Ruth Edwards
b. 1790
m. Richard Bennett

SABRINA BENNETT, 1817	m. Oliver Turner, 1857
Jeremiah Bennett, 1825	
Decatur Bennett, 1829	
Frances Bennett, 1833	

James Edwards
b. 1794   d. 1817
m. Alcemena Frisbee

*Persis Edwards	m. James Burnham

David Edwards
b. 1796
m. Alcemena (Frisbee) Edwards, 1819
- Eliza Edwards, 1819
- James Edwards, 1822
- John Edwards, 1824
- Statira Edwards, 1827
- Alcemena Edwards, 1830
- Almira Edwards, 1834

*Jemima Edwards
b. 1798
m. (1) John Blake
   (2) Daniel Sanborn[2]

*Ann Blake, 1828	m. William Lovejoy, 1853
Plummer Sanborn, 1821	m. Sarah Dearborn, 1844
Charles Sanborn, 1824	m. Parmelia Brown, 1850
Jane M. Sanborn, 1826	m. Jacob Martin, 1848
Luther Sanborn, 1829	m. Sarah Norris, 1856
Hannah Sanborn, 1831	m. Luther Rock, 1854

Hannah Edwards
b. 1801
m. John S. Bryant

Ann Byrant, 1823	m. Gardner Elliott, 1845
George Bryant, 1826	d. 1843
H. Louise Bryant, 1833	m. George Burleigh, 1854

Mary Edwards
b. 1806
m. Elias Colby
- Allen James Colby, 1845

*Malenda Edwards
b. 1809
m. James Blodgett

Sarah Edwards
b. 1812
m. Lewis Heath, 1832

Rufus Heath, 1833	d. 1842
Charles Heath, 1837	
Sarah Heath, 1841	
Frank Heath, 1845	
Nellie Heath, 1848	
George Heath, 1851	

---

1. Three children of John and Betsey Edwards who died before 1824 are excluded. Neither they nor any of their children figure in the letters.
2. All Sanborn children are from Daniel Sanborn's first marriage, not shown here.
* Letter writers included in this chapter are marked with asterisks.

TWO

Letters to Sabrina Bennett

SABRINA BENNETT, the oldest child of Richard and Ruth Edwards Bennett, lived in Haverhill, Massachusetts in the middle decades of the nineteenth century. There she maintained an extensive correspondence with numerous relatives across New England. Her cousins and aunts kept up a steady stream of letters, some written while they were single and working in Nashua and Lowell, others reflecting the patterns of their lives after marriage.[1] Sabrina stayed put in this period, the 1830s and 1840s, while her kin filled her in on work and travel and family developments. To our good fortune Sabrina saved these letters, permitting us a view of urban and rural alternatives open to New England women in the antebellum years.[2]

The letters are particularly useful in delineating the range of women's occupations in this period. Aunt Malenda Edwards and cousin Olive Sawyer Brown described women's farm chores including such diverse activities as dairying, spinning, weaving, and raking hay. Another group of cousins, Persis Edwards and Louisa, Emeline, and Hepzibah Sawyer, worked in textile mills in Nashua and Lowell. Finally, cousin Ann Blake worked as a dressmaker for a period, an occupation apparently followed by Sabrina Bennett as well. Of major women's occupations in these years only schoolteaching and urban domestic service are unrepresented.

What becomes most evident in these letters are the ways that women's decisions regarding employment and residence were intimately related to their place in the broader family economy. On several occasions single women deferred to their parents or revealed that they were motivated by a primary concern to support or care for their parents. Persis Edwards noted without complaint in her letter of April 18, 1840 that her mother

1. The accompanying family tree, "Sabrina Bennett and her Extended Kinship Network," notes the extensive Edwards clan, children and grandchildren of John and Betsy Edwards. Letter writers are indicated by asterisks.
2. Bennett Family Letters, Haverhill Public Library, Haverhill, Mass.

would not let her return to Nashua. Malenda Edwards moved between Bristol and Nashua during the period 1839-1845, supporting herself no doubt, but also taking care of her aged parents. She noted once that she was "physician and nurse" to her father and indicated that except for her parents' need for her she would have migrated west.[3]

The economic interdependence within the family economy is most clearly expressed in the letters of Jemima Sanborn who took half of her family to Nashua in the spring of 1843. Two sons remained on the family homestead in Bristol to keep up the farm and care for their grandparents, John and Betsy Edwards. Jemima Sanborn moved to nearby Nashua with three daughters and two sons.[4] Within a short time two daughters, Ann Blake and Jane Sanborn, were working at the Jackson Company. Her husband, Daniel Sanborn, seems to have moved back and forth between urban employment and farm work depending on immediate family needs. Urban life, however, did not appeal to Aunt Jemima and she complained to Sabrina Bennett: "I am as lonesome as you can think here among all strangers." Even though she was forty-four at this time and the mother of a sizable family she had difficulty leaving the family homestead. As she explained to Sabrina, "I never was weaned from fathers house before."[5]

While the letters to Sabrina Bennett present a rich view of options open to women in New England in the 1830s and 1840s, they are also a diverse and at times hard to follow collection. It may be helpful at the outset to describe the letter writers and introduce briefly the cast of characters these letters present. The letters reprinted below are arranged by author, there being five small sets in all. They are selected from a larger collection that includes occasional letters from Sabrina's male cousins and cousins-in-law. The women's letters predominate, however, and the selection process has not altered significantly the character of the surviving correspondence.

Olive and Louisa Sawyer, cousins of Sabrina Bennett, authored the first letters presented below. The sisters were daughters of Jeremiah and Hepzibah Edwards Sawyer of Canterbury, New Hampshire, and their letters provide contrasting views of women's lives. Olive lived at home until her marriage in 1838 to Simeon Brown when she moved to Franklin,

---

3. M.M. Edwards to Sabrina Bennett, Aug. 18, 1845, see below.
4. For simplicity I refer here to Jemima Sanborn's "daughters and sons." In point of fact, she had one daughter and five stepchildren. The Sanborn children were all from Daniel Sanborn's first marriage. See the accompanying chart, "Sabrina Bennett and her Extended Kinship Network."
5. Jemima Sanborn to Richard and Ruth Bennett, May 14, 1843, see below.

New Hampshire. There she took charge of the dairy, producing in one year 1,100 pounds of cheese and 400 pounds of butter from her herd of ten cows. Her sister, Louisa, by contrast, worked off and on in Lowell from 1836 to 1850 where she was joined periodically by her sisters, Emeline and Hepzibah, and her brothers, Daniel and Jeremiah. While her letters offer little about work or life in Lowell, they do reveal the existence of a strong kinship network that provided emotional support in the urban factory setting.

Cousin Persis Edwards and Aunt Malenda Edwards provide the next two sets of letters. They came together to Nashua in 1839 where they worked and boarded together. Persis returned home to her parents in Barnet, Vermont, and later married James Burnham. The new couple lived first in Houlton, Maine, on the Canadian border, and then moved to Andover, Massachusetts, where they were quite close to Sabrina Bennett in Haverhill. Malenda moved back and forth between work in Nashua and helping her parents in nearby Bristol. Finally, at the age of thirty-six, she married a coachmaker, James Blodgett, and moved to Concord. Her widowed mother resided with the couple after her father's death in 1849. Whether single or married, Malenda Edwards Blodgett assumed the roles of provider and caretaker toward her parents.[6]

The final letters in this section provide insights into the family economic strategies of Daniel and Jemima Edwards Sanborn. Covering a two-year period between 1843 and 1845, these letters show the motivations of a mother and her children as they coped with economic uncertainty in the years immediately following the depression of 1837-1842.

As we read portions of Sabrina Bennett's correspondence for the fifteen years covered here we wonder what her life must have been like. She appears to have been a dressmaker judging from comments in letters she received. But did she always remain so? We cannot be certain. At least one letter, written by James Burnham in May 1850, found Sabrina living in or visiting Lowell. Whether she ever succumbed to "mill fever" and entered factory employment is one of the many questions raised but left unanswered by these letters.

---

6. Richard W. Musgrove, *History of the Town of Bristol, Grafton County, New Hampshire* (Bristol: by the author, 1904), 2:163; 1850 Census of Concord, N.H., dwelling 585.

Letters of Olive Sawyer, 1836-1840

Canterbury Sabbath morning Sept the 25 1836

Dear Cousin,[7]

I now improve a few leisure moments in writing to you for the first time since you left NH. No doubt you will excuse me for not writing since I received your last when I tell that Samuel is very sick with Billious Fever.[8] He was taken a week ago yesterday. It goes very hard with him he says he dont think he ever shall get well again. He says he is willing to die if the lord will only prepare him. He was sick with the same fever in July last but it did not go so hard with him as it does now. He then promised the lord if he would restore him to health again he would seek religion. The lord see fit to raise him to health again but Samuel did not do as he promised [and] the lord has once more seen fit to lay his afflicting rod upon him. Once more has he laid him on a bed of languishing sickness. He says if he ever gets all well again he will live a Christian. O Sabrina universalism wont stand by in a dieing hour.[9] It is very sickly around here Fevers and dysentery is the general complaint. Hary Ladd died about one oclock this morning with the same Fever that Samuel has. Sarah Folsom has been very sick with the same but is like to recover. My health has been very poor for the most part of the time this sumer but is tolerable good at this time. Uncles and Aunts health is quite poor.

We received a letter yesterday from Rachel Frisbie.[10] They were all well. Charlotte is maried to her Garret was maried if I mistake not in May last. Rachel writes remember me to Miss Bennet. I would likewise inform you that Mrs. Rasford has a young son & his name is Franklin

7. This letter, like most in this collection, is addressed to Sabrina Bennett of Haverhill, Mass. The writer of this letter and of the next two is Olive Sawyer. Olive's mother, Hepzibah Edwards Sawyer, and Sabrina's mother, Ruth Edwards Bennett, are sisters. Musgrove, *History of Bristol*, 2:163.

8. From context Samuel would seem to be a brother, although he is not listed among the children of Jeremiah and Hepzibah Sawyer in either published genealogy. Musgrove, *History of Bristol*, 2:163; Ernest Bogart, *Peacham: The Story of a Vermont Hill Town* (Montpelier, Vt.: Vermont Historical Society, 1948), pp. 312-13.

9. Universalist ministers in this period argued for a concept of universal salvation quite at odds with the dominant Calvinist sentiments of most New Englanders, hence Olive Sawyer's comment here. Sydney Ahlstrom, *A Religious History of the American People* (New Haven: Yale University Press, 1972), pp. 481-83.

10. Rachel Frisbie is probably another cousin, daughter of Timothy Frisbie and the oldest of the Edwards daughters, Betsey.

Augustus. Esq. Tabor writes that he is a great fat boy, whole hog
Frisbie. Eliza has gone back to vermont.[11] She was so homesick she
sent word to her Father to come after her. The last I heard from Jane
Livingston she was well and contented and making good wages.
Catherine Edwards has gone to work in the Factory. Uncle Bryant and
aunt Hannah was down about two weeks ago.[12] Mothers health has
been very poor this summer. Louisa has come home from the Factory
she came home in June.[13] I am sorry to have you think that I am fixing
to get Maried. I will just tell you it is false. What reason have you to
think so I am sure I never gave you any. You asked if Tommy was the
happy man. I will answer he is not. Perhaps you will then ask if it is
Hoyt. I will answer it is not. That is not the cause of my hurry but I
will leave this subject for the present. I want to see you very much but
dont know when I shall. You wrote you wanted me to come to
Haverhill to work. I dont think i ever shall. Give my love to uncle
Lewis and aunt Sally and to Mr. Johnsons folks and all inquiring
friends.[14] Except [sic] the same to your self.

I have broke off rather short but never mind that i am rather tired. I
will now close my ill composed letter by wishing you good health and
prosperity. Write me back by your father.

yours with much respect

Olive Sawyer

Canterbury NH
I have filled this sheet and I want you to fill another. Write your
feelings. I have wrote mine.
ADIEU SABRINA
I expected when I wrote this to have sent it by your Father but I will
put in the mail. Your folks are well. Write as soon as you can.

---

11. Other letters suggest that this is Eliza Edwards, daughter of David and
Alcemena Frisbie Edwards of Newbury, Vt., another cousin of Olive Sawyer.
Frederic P. Wells, *History of Newbury, Vermont: From the Discovery of Coos County
to Present Time* (St. Johnsbury, Vt.: Caledonian Company, 1902), pp. 540-41.
12. Olive keeps in touch with quite an extended network of kin. Referred to
here are Uncle John S. Bryant and his wife, the former Hannah Edwards. The
Bryants lived in Bristol for a period in the 1820s and 1830s and moved to
Haverhill in the mid-1840s. Musgrove, *History of Bristol*, 2:72.
13. This is probably Louisa A. Sawyer, Olive's sister.
14. The relatives cited here would be Lewis Heath and Sally Edwards Heath
who were married in May 1832, lived in Haverhill for a period, and then
resided in Andover, N.H. Musgrove, *History of Bristol*, 2:233; 1850 Census of
Andover, dwelling 73.

Tuesday the 27

Sabrina,

I had sealed my letter but I broke it open to tell you the good tidings. Sabbath day Samuel was very much woried in his mind. We sent for deacon Mathis to come and pray with him. He come and praied with him. After he had done Samuel praied this was about four oclock PM but he found no relief of mind until about 9 oclock when the lord forgave his sins and he cried Glory to God Mother the Lord has heard my prayer. He called me to his bed side and told me to seek religion. O Sabrina I wish you had been here so that we could have wept together. It was a time of rejoicing. He was one of the most happy creatures I ever saw. He says he never knew what it was to be happy before he found religion. O he cant believe universilism now although he tried to last winter.

Your mother is here this afternoon she rejoices with Samuel to think that he is so happy. He is no better in health he is dangerously sick. Dr. Harper was here sunday he says it is a doubtful case. I should not think strange if he did not live till Saterday. If he dous not I will send you word. Let it not grieve your bosem no doubt but what it will but tears wont save him. I dont think but what I have shed a pint of tears. O Sabrina my heart aches while I pen these lines to you. I cant write any more. So adieu

Olive Sawyer

Franklin[15] May the 15 1839

Dear Cousin

After a period of rather more then twelve months I again take my pen to communicate afew lines to you after making a few apoliges for my negligence. In the first place it was because I had not received an answer to my last and in the next it was because I knew not where to direct a letter.

But having once more heard from my dear Cos I will try for the future and not be so neglecful. My health has been quite good the most of the time since I last wrote although it is not so good at present as usual though I have no reason to complain for it is through the divine mercies of God that I am alive and able to address you. I am

15. Franklin, N.H., is located in the northern tip of Merrimack County, about fifteen miles from Canterbury. It is only eight miles south of Bristol, the home of John and Betsey Edwards, who were heads of the extensive Edwards clan.

very sorry that you are so unfortunate as to be deprived of your health for without health life seems to be wearysome. You wanted I should tell you how I like the maried state.[16] I will tell you that I never enjoyed myself so well in my life as I have since I have been married. I have one of the kindest husbands that ever a woman had and that is to be prefered before riches. I have enough of every thing to eat and to drink though I dont live in the style and the fashions of the gay and noble. I live in the woods among the stumps and owls. I have not as yet Cos had any addition to the famiely so you will have to suppose again. I have but[ter] & cows this summer. I had 10 [cows] last year. I made eleven hundred weight of new milk Cheese [and] 4 hundred of butter beside considerable skim milk cheese. We raised six calves which made quite and [sic] addition to our stock. I will now leave this subject. Fathers folks are all well Mother was here Monday. She had been to cary Hepsy and emeline to Franklin village to take the stage for Lowell.[17] Louisa has been there over a year and they are all there now. It was quite a mistake about Mr Sargents Brother being partial to either of them. Jeremiah lives at home with Father he is quite an altered young man. He has lately been converted and baptised. We some expect he will be married this fall to a girl by the name of Badger.

Fathers folks are prospering finely. They have got a beautiful place. Jerey expects to live with them. He says he should be very glad to have you write him and then he will endevor to write to you. Mother said she meant to write to uncle and aunt. She sends her best respects to them and the rest of the family. Hepsy wants you to write to her. I will just say that I have not been to Bristol since you went with me nor have not seen one of them although they have been to Andover but did not come here.[18] I wish you would come up this summer for I do want to see my Cousin once more. I should be very glad to visit you

16. Olive Sawyer married Simeon Brown in 1838. The couple moved to Franklin where Olive died in 1841. Bogart, *Peacham*, p. 313.

17. Hepzibah and Emeline are two sisters of Olive. Lowell proved attractive to almost all of the Sawyer children. Daniel, Jeremiah, and Louisa also worked there, as subsequent letters reveal. Surviving company records reveal that two of the daughters worked at the Hamilton Company. Hepzibah had four stints at the company in the carding and weaving rooms between 1835 and 1840; Louisa worked off and on at the Hamilton and Lawrence companies at least between 1835 and 1841. Hamilton Manufacturing Company records, vols. 483, 485, 486, Baker Library, Harvard Business School.

18. Andover lies about eight miles due west of Franklin. The main route from Bristol to Andover goes through Franklin.

Waiting for the Stage Coach, 1834. Oil Painting by Alvan Fisher.

Courtesy of Old Sturbridge Village and New Britain Museum of American Art.

this fall if i Could but it will not be Convinient. Give my love to your
Pa and Ma and the same to yourself. Write again soon and direct your
letters to Simeon Brown.

Olive Brown

Give my love to uncle and aunt Heath.

> Tis not the distance of the place
> Nor yet the lenght [*sic*] of time
> Tis not the absence of your face
> Shall keep you from my mind.

Franklin [N.H.] November the 14 1840

Dear Cos,

I take my pen this eve with feelings to painful to describe to inform
you of the death of my beloved brother Jeremiah. He died in Lowell
the 14 of October with the Typhus Fever. Yes dear Sabrina he is gone
no more to return to us but we must meet him sooner or later. You
must expect dear Cousin that we are in trouble here. It has almost
undone Father and Mother. They were making great dependence upon
him in there old age. It seems as though we could not be reconciled to
it but we must say with one of old the Lords will not mine be done.

He went from house the 23rd of March to Quincy Mass[achusetts]
with one of my husbands brothers. [He] intended to have workd there
through the season but the work was to hard for his lame hand. He left
there and went to Lowell. He worked there about 5 months when he
was taken sick and died. Hepsy and Louisa were there with him
through his sickness. He had the best care and attention that he could
have. They wrote to Father as soon as they considered him dangerous.
Mother started for Lowell as soon as they got the letter. She went
through in one day but before she got there he was dead and buried.
All my dear Mother could see was the little spot where [he] was laid.
He was all mortified so that that they could not bring him home. It cost
all he had earned this summer and more to[o]. Sister H[epzibah] paid
his Doctors bill out of her own wages. There never was two sisters that
ever done better by a brother than they did. He was crazy through his
sickness till eleven hours before he died. He had his reasons he was
one of the happiest creatures that ever was: O said he that Religion
that was my comfort in health is my support now. He longed to go and
be with his Saviour. About fifteen minutes before he died he sang two

verses of Alas and did my Saviour bleed with a loud and clear voice.[19] O Cousin it was trouble we knew nothing about.

I will now give you a sketch of my own family which are all about at this time. My little son has been sick ever since the first of August. He has not seen awell minute since he was taken with the dysentary in the first place which run him all down to a mere skeliton. He got better of that and then his teeth cut very hard which kept him in a diarea. Well within ashort time he has began to pick up his crumbs again and if nothing more befalls him I think he will recover again. It has been a season of confinement to me. I will assure you we intended to have made a journey to the salt water this fall but sickness prevented. I was very sorry to hear of your ill health likewise your Father and Mothers. Hope you will recover and take a journey to New Hampshire this winter. My health is quite good this fall. Father folks are well. Emeline and Daniel are at home. E[meline] has got to be a great girl she is Ful larger than Mother. H[epzibah] and L[ouisa] are in Lowell, John is in Boston. He was Maried this fall to a lady in B[oston]. Her name was Phebe Ann Fields. I some expect they will be up this winter. H[epzibah] expects to be Married in the spring.

Louisa will spend the winter in L[owell]. She is a fine girl. Do Cousin write to her she would be very glad to have you. I have writen all the news and now I will Close for Simeon says do come to bed Olive. You must forgive all mistakes and write as soon as you can.

receive this from your long absent
Cousin Olive S B [Sawyer Brown]

Letters of Louisa Sawyer, 1849-1850

[Lowell, December ?, 1849][20]

Cousin Sabrina,

After so long a time I again seat myself to address a line to you. It is a long time since I have seen or heard from you but believing I am not forgotten I will chatt awhile this eve with you. Would you like to know what I have been doing? For a long time I would say I have been

19. "Alas and Did My Saviour Bleed" is the first line of a hymn written by the famous English nonconformist minister, Isaac Watts. John Julian, A Dictionary of Hymnology (New York: Dover, 1957; originally published in 1892), 1:34.
20. Comments within this letter permit one to infer the place and date of writing. Louisa remained in Lowell through June 1850 as she was enumerated in a company boardinghouse, dwelling 1199.

Home for abbout ten weeks just. Mothers health was very poor when I first went home but she was smart before I came away. I enjoyed myself very much while thare what a beautifull [letter torn] we have had. It was delightfull in the country, I asshure you I never enjoyed myself better. We had greate times in [go]ing to Apple bees or rather Punkim [pumpkin] bees for there were not many Apples this year. I did not visit our friends in Bristol but Farther and Mother did while I was at home. They were well. Mr Blodgets folks have moved to Concord and Granmother has left the good old Farm and consented to be shut up thare with them.[21] I do not think she will live very long to enjoy their nice House. Cousin Ann Blake is about getting married.[22] She is going out very well they say he is a very smart young man. Cousin Sabrina it is so long since I saw you that I hardly know what to say. What I write you will perceive will be mostly stems a Little hear and there. Mother received a letter from Aunt Mary Colby.[23] She was well and hur family. She dose not like the proceedings at all in regard to Granfarthers property and I guess she will make a fuss and I hope she will get what belongs to hur. I should think by what she wrote that she held a not[e] for quite a sum against that prope[r]ty. Melinda [Edwards Blodgett] ought to pay what is due I think and I guess she will be oblidged to yet. I should not wondr if Unkle David [Edwards] made quite a stir with them or at least with JS Bryant but no more of this.

Well Cousin I am again in Lowell and think I shall work in the Mill this winter and dont know how much longer. Sister Emeline is here. Hur health is very good. We think of visiting Haverhill this Winter if nothing prevents.[24] I hope I shall have the pleasure of seeing you here this winter and your Brothers. I want to see you all very much. Please give my Love to your Farther and Mother and Frances and to all who inquire after me. We had a very pleasant time at Thanksgiving enjoyed myself very much. I had the pleasure of haveing two days to *be*

21. This is James S. Blodgett, husband of Malenda Edwards. John Edwards had died in January 1849 and, as this letter notes, grandmother Betsy moved to Concord and lived with James and Malenda Blodgett; see 1850 Census of Concord, dwelling 585.

22. Ann Blake is the daughter of Jemima Edwards Sanborn—Aunt Jemima in later letters—by her first marriage. Despite the expectation expressed here, she did not marry until May 1853. Musgrove, *History of Bristol*, 2:292.

23. This is Mary Edwards Colby, another of the Edwards sisters. She and her husband soon set off for Oregon and she wrote a lengthy account of her experience on the journey. See Bennett Family Letters.

24. Haverhill was only about fifteen miles further down the Merrimack River from Lowell.

Hamilton Company, Lowell, where the Sawyer sisters worked, 1835–1850.

thankfull for. Brother Daniel and myself came here the night before the 29. He would have visited you if he could [have] left his business any longer. I expect him down again soon and he will then visit you. He is well and you would hardly know him he grows so. He is as steady young man as I know of. Cousin Sabrina I will not weary your patiance in writing eny longer at this time and so I will bring these scribblings to a close and will say answer this as so[o]n as you receive this and write all the news. Please write about Mr Busshorns folks and all the news you can think of Cousin. I am going to send this by a Lady that boards with me. She is going to spend some time in Haverhill to a Brothers that lives thare. She is going to be married this week. She is a fine Lady and you would like to get acquainted with her I think. Her name is Sage. Good night write soon. From your cousin
Louisa A. Sawyer
Lowell Mass

[East Andover, N.H., Dec. 30, 1850]

Cousin Sabrina,

It is Sabbath morning in Newhampsire and I thought perhaps you would like to know how we are prospering in this Snow Clad region. In the first place I will tell you from living since I started for Hampshire two weeks ago last Wendsdy. I arrived in Concord and stayed one day had a very pleasant time found our friends all well though I think Granmother is failing fast.[25] She was quite comfortable for hur but I do not think she will stay very long with us. They are very pleasantly situated. I think Concord is a very pleasant place. Cousin Ann Blake boards thare and works in a shop. She is not married yet and she dose not seem to be in a very greate hurry. She seems to enjoy hur self very well. Jane lives thare and is very pleasently situated. She has got one of the prettyest babys that you ever saw. She calls it Clara Jainy.[26] I arrived at my own Little Home and found the folks all well and here I am domesticated and having a good time. Brother Daniel came Home yestody and is well and left the Lowell friends all well. Sister Emeline dose not think of comeing Home to stay this winter. It seemed rather lonely when I first came Home it

25. Actually Betsey Edwards lived another four and a half years, dying in July 1855. Musgrove, *History of Bristol*, 2:163.
26. By this date a number of the Edwards clan are living in Concord. They include Jane Sanborn Martin, stepsister of Ann Blake, and her first child, Clara Jane, born in August 1850. Musgrove, *History of Bristol*, 2:300, 369.

was so still and quiet but it seems now very pleasant and I antisipate having a very pleasant time. We have a very flourshing school abbout 50 schollars. We have a Lernin and Singing School and the Sleigh kids you better believe and I rather guess the young folks and Old Bachelrs know how to enjoy life the old fashion way. Enoch Osgood ses he should like to see the Haverhill folks very well. Cousin Sabrina if there is eny chance for speculation this winter I shall speak for a steady chance for having a *spare hands chance* I dont think much of it.[27] I should like very much to see some of my Haverhill and Lowell friends and have a chatt with them. Please give my line to Mr Stevens and wife and tell him I have not seen eny of his folks but Father has and they are well. Give my line to your brothers and tell them to get a sleigh some moonlight eveni[n]g and all Hands to come up here. Unkle David started for Vermont the day I came Home did not see them they took the cars from here.[28] Give my line to Frank and Mrs Goffield and tell him to send me some papers. Well Cousin I have written more now than I guess will be interresting so I will close by saying write as soon as you get this and tell me all the news. So good by, from your

Cousin
Louisa A. Sawyer

Daniel sends a pocket full of Lines.

Frank, you must be a good Girl and mind your mother and ceap thoes curls combed and strait.[29] My best love to Jer[e]miah and Decater also to Sabrina.

From your Cousin D[aniel] E. Sawyer

Letters of Persis Edwards, 1839-1850

Nashua April 4 1839

My Dear Cousin,

Doubtless you will be suprised to hear from me as I am not in the habit of holding correspondence with you. It is not because I have forgotten you no, Dear S. I often think of you & could as often wish to

27. Louisa uses language from the mills here. A "sparehand" was the lowest-paid worker in the job hierarchy of the mills. When a woman first entered the mills, she would be hired as a sparehand with no assurance of a regular job, but with hope of placement in a better position if another worker left. Hence the term, a "sparehand's chance."

28. David Edwards would have taken the Northern Railroad north to White River Junction, just across the New Hampshire-Vermont border.

29. Daniel Sawyer writes this postscript. He refers in the paragraph to Sabrina's siblings. Frank is sister Frances, seventeen at this date. Jeremiah,

see you. I suppose I need not apolygize for past negligence as you are guilty of the same yourself. I hope we shall let past neglig[en]ce suffice & for the future commence a correspondence. There shall be no lack on my part. I have often thought of you since I came to this place & especially since I heard that you was obliged to give up your shop on account of ill health. I left Vermont last july came to Bristol & stayed until October when I came to this place.[30] I work in the mill like very well enjoy myself much better than I expected. [I] am very confined could wish to have my liberty a little more but however I can put up with that as I am favored with other priveleges. I think I shall visit you this Summer. I think if nothing in providence prevents I shall stay here untill fall. It seems now a long time since I left home am almost homesick sometimes. I heard from home last week & likewise from Bristol. Our folks all & Grandfarthers are all in good health except Aunt Bryant she has not been able to work this winter.

I will just say I hope you will answer this soon. Give my love to uncle & Aunt & all friends. If you do not think of coming here to work I hope [you come] & visit us. I want to see you very much hope to soon. Write us all the news you have & believe [me] to be [your] undeviating Friend & Cousin

Persis L. Edwards

[April 4, 1839][31]

Dear Sabrina,

I have nothing special to write you but Persis has commenced a letter [and] I will try and think of something if it is not so very interesting. You have been informed I supose that I am a factory girl and that I am at Nashua and I have wished you were here too but I suppose your mother would think it far beneith your dignity to be a factory girl.[32] Their are very many young Ladies at work in the factories that have given up milinary d[r]essmaking & s[c]hool keeping

twenty-four, and Decatur, twenty-two, are both recorded as shoemakers living at home with their parents in the 1850 Census of Haverhill, family 554. Sabrina, thirty-three, is the oldest of the children still living at home.

30. She has probably come from Newbury, Vt., home of her likely stepfather and mother, David and Alcemena Edwards.

31. This letter was mailed with the previous one and is dated accordingly. It was written by Malenda Edwards, several of whose later letters appear below.

32. Sabrina's mother, Ruth Edwards Bennett, is Malenda's sister. The language used here is common; although Malenda is twenty-nine years old, she refers to herself as a "factory girl."

for to work in the mill. But I would not advise any one to do it for I was so sick of it at first I wished a factory had never been thought of. But the longer I stay the better I like and I think if nothing unforesene calls me away I shall stay here till fall. Persis has told you that the folks at Bristol were all well but sister Bryant and I fear if she does not get help soon she never will be any better. Your uncle Frisbies folks have moved to New York where his Brother lives. Your uncle [Daniel] Sandborn has buried his father he died the 4 of March. Give my respects to your fathers folks and except [sic] much love your self from me. Write soon and write me all the news you can think. I want to hear from Haverhill. Write too where you are and what you are doing and what you intend to do this summer. My health is very poor indeed but it is better than it was when I left home. If you should have any idea of working in the factory I will do the best I can to get you a place with us. We have an excelent boarding place. We board with a family with whome I was acquainted with when I lived at Haverhill. Pleas to write us soon and believe your affectionate Aunt

M[alenda] M. Edwards

Barnet [Vt] April the 18 1840

My very Dear Coussin,

I received your letter dated jan. 24 after a long time it layed in the office. Be assured it met with the most hearty welcome was read over & over again & again. It brought to mind the many social hours we have spent together which are now past. You said in your letter shall we ever have the pleasure of seeing & conversing with each other again. Could I answer, it would be in the affirmitive. I can only say this much I sincerely hope to & that ere long. I had about given up the idea of having any friends untill I received your letter had not received any since I came home. Have found there is one which has not forgotten me although I do not deserve to be held in remembrance by you. Dear S[abrina] I do feel as though I had not done right. I should have written before I left N[ashua] but neglected one oppertunity after another by that means did not write at all. I would apologize much were it not in vain, hope you will excuse me for this time, will make amends for the future. I anticipated much happiness in visiting you last Summer hope you will not think hard of me for not coming. [I] could hardly be persuaded to give up the idea intended to have gone in june. Aunt Malinda wis[h]ed me to wait until September she said then she would go with me. I consented rather than to go alone. She then soon give up about coming at all. I think much about seeing you wish I

Newbury, Vermont scene, c. 1850.
Hometown of Persis Edwards' family after 1843.

Courtesy of Shelburne Museum, Shelburne, Vermont.

could visit you this summer am now at home. When I came here last fall found Sister E[liza] confined with the Fever. She recovered in a few weeks then Mother & Alcemena were confined at a time & myself likewise. After we got better Almira & John they got about then James was sick about three weeks.[33] The first day of january Father froze his foot was not able to work for five or six weeks. The first day he went to work, the boys went into the woods with him to chop wood. James cut his foot was not able to go to school for three weeks & so we have had one trouble after another ever since I came home till this Spring. We are now all enjoying good health, which above every thing else we should be thankful for. I feel as though it was through the Goodness & Mercy of God that we are spared. It can surely be nothing that we merit from our own goodness.

Sister E[liza] is not at home is now living at Walden will return home soon. We expect next week to move about a mile from where we now live. Father can have more land to carry on than he can here. I hardly know what to tell you about the Society here, have become but a very little acquainted. What acquaintance I have formed is very pleasant have felt very lonesome since I came home. Judge if you please what your feeling would have been had you been placed in the same situation I have for six months past & strangers too excepting your Fathers family. I do not wish too neither will I murmur at the hand of Providence, can but drop a tear as I now write you. Would that you were here methinks you would simpathise with me. I do not know what my employment will be this summer. Mother is not willing I should go to the Factory. I thought some of learning the Milleners & Dressmakers trade but have failed in the attempt. I wrote to Uncle Bryants folks to know if I could get in there to Haverhill cannot under four or five months [p]ay my own board cannot do that. They thought it would be rather incovenient for them to board me if I could get in. You may well know the reason I am not popular. Cousin Ann [Blake] is the top of Haverhill Corner she had a Broadcloth cloak last winter cost over 30 dollars.

If I could learn the trade there is a very pleasant village in this town which would be a good place to work. There is no one in the place

33. The individuals listed here are all children of David and Alcemena Edwards and are cousins of Sabrina. Genealogies of the family do not list Persis but I infer from them and the letters that she is the daughter of James and Alcemena Edwards. Her father died in 1817 and when her mother married his brother, David Edwards, in 1819, Persis was simply raised as a member of the family. Wells, *History of Newbury*, pp. 540-41. See the genealogical chart at the outset of this section.

that keeps shop. Hope you will try to visit us this summer. Come & spend a long time with us. Write to me as soon as you get this tell me of your Prosperity & how you are employed dont delay. If you work at your trade I should be glad to work with you. I wish you were here in a shop could you come we should enjoy all the pleasure imaginable. Father & Mother send love to your Parents wish them to visit us as soon as convenient. Give them my love.

My Brothers & Sisters all send love to you all, you have our best wishes for your Prosperity. Cousin there shall be no lack on my part about keeping up a correspondence. Answer this as soon as possible direct your letter to Peacham. Barnet Post Office is five miles from us. Believe me to remain your very affectionate Cousin

Persis L Edwards

Houlton[34] August 23, 1846

Dear Cousin,

Agreeable to promise I will write you a few lines, although I am rather late in the day about it. I trust you will excuse me for neglect as I have had so many other things to take up my attention since I returned home. I send this by Aunt Mary [Edwards]. She & Adin & wife will start for Haverhill tomorrow morning.

We hope you & your folks will excuse us for not visiting you on our return. We had been absent so long we could not spend any more time with you. We found Mother very poorly was very sick when we were there had ten fits, they are very distressing. I think they have injured her greatly she hardly appeared natural. We spent about two weeks at home wished to spend all the time with Mother possible.

Sister Eliza was at home to spend a short time. Her husband was in Hartford the rest of our family were at home & very well.

Grandfather Edwards & Grandmother were very smart. Aunt Malinda [Edwards] was published before we left for home. We did not see her intended.[35] Uncle Nick [Daniel] Sandborn was very poorly. When we were there [he] was obliged to walk with a crutch. Aunt [Jemima] was taken sick on the road before they reached home was confined to her bed some time.

34. By this date Persis has married James Burnham and is residing in Houlton on the extreme eastern boundary of Maine.

35. Malenda Edwards's "intended" is probably James Blodgett. The marriage date is uncertain, but the couple was married by early 1849 as Louisa Sawyer's earlier letter indicates.

Mr. Burnham is settling up his business at the store intends to leave Houlton before a long time do not know where we shall go. I wish I did. If I could come on somewhere near you I should like it. I suppose John [Frisbie] is married before this.[36] Did you not go to the wedding? Write me & tell me all about it every particular. My love to your Mother & Father Brothers & Sister. Tell them I want to see them all. Tell Grandmother Frisbee I wish her much joy with her new Daughter. Remember us to John & wife tell them I wish all the happines imaginable. Write to us very soon. Will let you know when we are going to leave Houlton as soon as Mr Burnham makes up his mind shall not for several weeks yet want you to answer this before we leave.

from your affectionate Cousin

Persis L Burnham

Sabrina E Bennett
Haverhill
I like to have forgoten to say my little Willie is very smart begins to run alone.[37]

Andover[38] December 14 [1848]

Dear Cousin,

I am going to trouble you again with my scribling. Have patience & I will not weary you. We are all very well & doing about as well as we know how to do. Sister Alcemena is with us. She came the first of November. Ann Blake spent a week with us before Thanksgiving. She is now in Lawrence taking care of her intended husband. He is sick with a fever. He lives in Lawrence owns a livery stable is said to be a very smart fellow. They are to be married soon. Mary Jane is now a married woman she was married the 20 of November.[39] They went to Rode Island on a marriage tour. They wished very much to have us go with them but we could not. On their return they stoped & made us a

36. John Lafayette Frisbie, son of Betsey Edwards and Timothy Frisbie, is another cousin of Sabrina Bennett. He also worked in Lowell for a period, at the Tremont Company in 1845. Musgrove, *History of Bristol*, 2:163. Lafayette Frisbie to Sabrina Bennett, April 20, May 9, 1845, Bennett Family Letters.
37. This would be the Burnhams' only child, William, now probably about a year old. 1850 Census of Andover, Mass., dwelling 145.
38. The Burnhams have moved to Andover, Mass., since their last letters, and are now only about ten miles from Haverhill.
39. Mary Jane is probably Jane Sanborn, another cousin, who married Jacob Martin Nov. 25, 1848. Musgrove, *History of Bristol*, 2:369.

visit. I did not enjoy it much I was sick a bed, had a turn of the Cholera morbus.

Louisa Bryant is in Boston taking musick lessons will spend three months in the City.[40] We are expecting her here to make us a visit soon. I believe I have told you all the news I can think of & perhaps you knew it all before. Come & see us as soon as you can. I think you might have come before this time. Love to all. Alcemena sends love to all. She will be over as soon as she can. Write & let us know how you are getting along. I am expecting every day to hear you are going to [get] married there is so much of a stir about the matter. O I like to have forgotten to tell you Lou Bryant is engaged to John Stul an Orthodox minister in South Wobourn & Ann Elliott has a daughter.[41] I must close. Sister is waiting to take this to the Office so no more this time,

from Persis L Burnham

Andover Dec. the 16

Dear Cousin,

I will try to answer your letter was very glad to hear from you. I am not very smart to day feel hardly able to sit up. I have not heard anything in particular about your getting married. Ann said she heard you was going to be married. She heard nothing in particular about it. I told her I thought it must be a mistake I do not know why L[ouisa] Bryant & Nicols did not hold on. I suppose she had rather have a minister.

I should like to have you come over any time. I may not have a tea party till the first of next month but hardly think it will be long by my feelings. Alcemena would like & come to visit you if I could get along without her. She will come as soon as she can. I can not say much but come when you can & all the rest. Love to all. Shall send this by Decatur.[42] We were very glad to see him so no more. Alcemena sends love to all.

from Persis L B[urnham]

40. Louisa Bryant, another cousin, is the daughter of John and Hannah Edwards Bryant. Musgrove, *History of Bristol*, 2:73.
41. Ann Bryant married Gardner Elliott on Sept. 23, 1845. Musgrove, *History of Bristol*, 2:73.
42. Sabrina's brother is apparently visiting the Burnhams and carries Persis's letter with him back to Haverhill.

Andover [Mass.] May 27/50

Cosin S[abrina]

I received your letter this after noon & with Joy I write you to let you know that Persis is a grate deal better. You canot think how thankful I feel to Divine Providence for his goodness in thus sparing her to me and her little ones for what should I have done if she had been taken away. I can hardly bare to think of it. We have sent our Babe away from home, poor thing it seems hard to have to do so but it is better of[f] than it could be at home.[43]

I hope this wil find your cos better & you the same. If you see Miss Sawyer I wish to be rem[em]bered and say to her I hope she will forgive us for not writing an answer to hers sometime since. P[ersis] does not know that I am writing this but it is all the same. Aunty Betsey is at our ho[u]se now. We had a letter from Alcemena last week she is well but Elisa is not very smart. All the rest are well as usual.

I hope you will call and see us when you come from Lowell.[44] Persis would like to see you.

But I must close for want of time. Hope you can read this.

Yours in haste

Jas. P. Burnham

To S. E. Bennett

Tell Miss Sawyer I should like to see her.[45] If she will come over I will pinch her once or twice just to accomodate.

JPB

Letters of Malenda Edwards, 1842-1845

Bristol [N.H.] Feb 23 1842[46]

Absent friends,

Having a few leisure moments this afternoon, I sit down to write a few lines but do not know whether I can write any thing that will very

43. The Burnhams' "Babe" here would have been Anna, born Jan. 19, 1850. Massachusetts Bureau of Vital Records.

44. After receiving so many letters from cousins in Nashua and Lowell, it appears that Sabrina Bennett was working in Lowell at this date. By June, however, she seems to have been back in Haverhill, as the census recorded her living at home with her parents.

45. James Burnham may be referring to Emeline or Louisa Sawyer; both worked in Lowell in 1850. See Louisa Sawyer to Sabrina Bennett, Dec. 30, 1850, above.

46. Malenda Edwards is living with her parents at this date. The next three letters describe her work in Nashua and Bristol; later she marries James Blodgett and settles in Concord, N.H.

much interest you. We are all in usual health at this time but mother she has a very lame side but is able to be up most of the time. Daniel and his wife have just got home from Vermont and Haverhill the folks their [sic] are well. We have had a very pleasant winter thus far but not much sleighing or we should have visited you long before this. Charles Sandborn and Mary and myself have been talking of coming down all winter but we shall be under the necessity of giving it up at present but Sabrina I will tell you what we want.[47] Mary or I want to come to Haverhill and spend the summer if you think we can get a good chance and good wages. If Mary comes she will want to do housework or nursing. Mary says if Mrs. Sweet will give her nine shillings a week she will come and live with her.[48] If I come I should like to sew & will go out by the day or go into some family as seemstress or go into a milliners shop just which way you think I can do best. Now Sabrina if you will get either of us a place and send us word we will be OPH [?] like a broken jug handle. I suppose that fate has destined me to be an Old maid and it will therefore be necessary for me to find some place to locate for a while. I had a kind of a spark 4 or 5 weeks ago but they could not exactly come it upon this child and would not if they could.[49] We received a letter from John Sawyer a few weeks since which informed us of the death of his wife.[50] She left a little daughter how old I do not know not many days however.

Sabrina, mother says tell S to ask her father and mother if they have not forgotten that they have a poor old father and mother in the world. She thinks if they had not they would try to come and see them. Your Aunt Heath has buried her little Rufuss. He died in January his death was caused by geting hurt at school.

I do not know as I can think of any thing more to write at this time and I presume you will be glad unless it was written and composed better but you will excuse it when I tell you I am talking all the while I am writing. We should be very glad to have any and all of you come and see us and it seems to me you might if you would make an effort. Write to us S[abrina] as soon as you can get us a place. Write all the particulars about it and we will one of us be along soon. Give our

47. Charles Sanborn is Malenda's nephew, stepson of her sister, Jemima Edwards Sanborn. Another sister, Mary Edwards, remains single and lives with her parents.
48. Nine shillings at this time were equal to $1.50, a good wage for a domestic who would also have received room and board.
49. Read "spark" to mean "beau" or "date."
50. John Sawyer, Olive and Louisa's brother, was a nephew of Malenda Edwards.

respects to our friends at Haverhill and accept much love for your selves.

Malenda M Edwards

I like to have forgotten Plumer in my letter. He is now at Hill at school.[51] The school closes this week and then he is going to Haverhill NH to school, a smart fellow he.

———

Nashville Dec 22 1844[52]

Absent friends,

According to promis I should have written to you long before this and in fact I did write and waited for Mrs Sandborn to write till you heard from us by the way of John Frisbie and so have neglected to send till now.

I staid out of the mill two weeks sick at the time you was here and have been well ever since.[53] Me health was never better then it is now. When we last heard from Bristol which was a week or two since our folks were all well. Father has not been so smart for a year or too as he has been this fall. Mother['s] health is good for her. Her nose troubles her some but it is no worse than it has been. I recieved a letter from Mary [Edwards Colby] since you was here. Thay were well when thay wrote. She said her little Frances Ann had been sick with the croup but was better.[54] The rest of our friends are well as far as I know. Persis is married to a Mr. Burnham at Houlton she has not been home yet. I dont no how long I shall stay here but I think I shall go home some time in March. Father talks of letting out his farm next year and if he does I shall have to go home and see to things. I intend if it is possible to visit you before I go home. Charles is at Bristol now. Mr. Sandborn folks are pretty well all but Jane she has a bad cold and sore throat.

51. Plummer Sanborn is another nephew, stepson of Malenda's sister Jemima Sanborn, also resident in Bristol. Hill, N.H., is about three miles south of Bristol.

52. Nashville was a mill village adjoining Nashua, N.H. Malenda Edwards worked at the Jackson Company and boarded with Daniel Sanborn, according to the *Nashua Directory* for 1845. See also Jemima Sanborn to Sabrina Bennett, May 14, 1843, below.

53. Illness proved a real problem for women in the early mills since they received no sick pay. Some women wrote to their families asking that someone come and bring them home since they could not afford to pay room and board. Since Malenda was living with her sister, Jemima Sanborn, she could wait out her illness and then return to work.

54. Since Malenda's last letter, Mary Edwards has married Elias Colby. Musgrove, *History of Bristol*, 2:163.

Mr. Sandborn has been quite unwell but is better now. Thay send love to all. Ann [Blake] sends love to uncle aunt and cousins and we all hope you Sabrina and Jeremiah and Decator will visit us this winter. Please to accept much love from

Malenda M Edwards

Bristol [N.H.] Aug 18 1845

Dear Sabrina,

We received your letter sent by Mr Wells and I embrace the first opportunity to answer it and will now confess that I am a tremendous lazy corespondent at the best—and betwene my house work and da[i]ry spining weaving and raking hay I find but little time to write so I think I have appologised sifficiently for not writing you before this. I am very glad indeed you have been so kind to write us so often this summer for I am always glad to hear from absent friends if I cannot see them. I think it was a kind providence that directed my steps to Haverhill last winter for it is not likely that I shall visit you again so long as father and mother live if I should live for so long for they fail fast especially father.[55] He has had quite a number of ill turns this summer and I have been physician and nurse too. Dont you think Sabrina it is well I have taken some lessons in the line of phisick? Mother is able to do but little this sumer [compared] to what she has been sumers past. The warm wether overcomes her very much but we get a long first rate. I have got the most of my wool spun and two webs wove and at the mill and have been out and raked hay almost every afternoon whilst they were haying. Father did not have but two days extra help about his haying and we have not had a moments help in the House. Mother commenced spinning this summer with great speed and thought she should do wonders but she only spun 17 skeins and gave it up as a bad bargain. We recieved a letter from Brother and Sister Colby about 3 weeks ago. They are well and prospering nicely. They have a young son born in May last. Thay call his name Allen James for his two uncles. They bought a half lot of land and built them a house four good rooms on the ground and paid for it. Then they bought the other half lot with a good brick house on it and Mary says if we will just step in we may see Elias and Molly with thare two pretty babies in thare own brick house almost as grand as Lawyer

---

55. Malenda's father, John Edwards, actually lived another three and a half years. Musgrove, *History of Bristol*, 2:163.

Bryants folks.[56] O Sabrina how my western fever rages. Were it not for my father and mother I would be in the far west ere this summer closes but I shall not leave them for friends nor foes! Mary and Elias say Liz dont get married for you must come out here. I shall take up with thare advice unles I can find some kind hearted youth that want a wife and mother, one that is good looking and can hold up his head up. Then when all that comes to pass I am off in a fit of matrimony like a broken jug handle but till I find such an one I glory in being an old maid, ha ha ha! Lewis Heath was here last saturday. Sally [Edwards Heath] has a young son to[o]. She is quite smart. Mr Sawyers folks are as well as usual. We have heard nothing from Davids since they were here. Ann Bryant is to be married the 26 of Sept the wedding will go off and a Splendid party follow. Daniels folks are well. Miriam ann and Jane went to Gilmanton last week the people are well and also our friends. Mr Sibley is not Dead as you heard. Aunt Sally is not married but is at Capt Norises spining and weaving this summer, that Old Lady 77 years old.[57]

I do not think of any more news to write as it is late and I am tired and some what sick so I will lay this aside till a more convenient time. This morning I fainted away and had to lay on the shed flour [*sic*] fifteen or twenty minutes for any comfort before I could get to the bed. And to pay for it tomorow I have got to wash churn, bake and make a chese and go over to Daniels blackber[ry]ing. So good night.

Tuesday   We have accomplished our task to day all but going blackber[ry]ing and it is so tremendous hot I dare not venture out so far. Father and mother wish to be rememberd to your folks and to all of Uncle Williams folks. They say it is not likely they shall ever visit Haverhill again and that they should be glad to se[e] any of you here that can come. We are disappointed in not seeing your father and mother here this sumer. Tell them if ever you[r] mother is well enough to perform the journey they must ceartainly come and see us. Father says he shall expect uncle this fall. I am sory to hear that John Frisbee is sick so much but the most of us know what it is to be sick by experience, for one I do and know what it is to earn money by hard labour to pay my Dr bills and other expenses at home and abroad. How sudden and unexpected Cosen William family has been broken up. It seems too much to think of or to realise that it is so and we know not whose turn will come. Remember me to your father and

56. "Lawyer Bryant's folks" would have been the parents of John S. Bryant, Malenda's brother-in-law, who practiced law in Haverhill.
57. The identity of "Aunt Sally" is uncertain, but at seventy-seven years of age she was probably a sister of either John or Betsey Edwards.

mother Brothers and sister. Write as often as you find time and also to the rest of our friends in H[averhill] and all enquirers. Tell Mrs. Frisbee that I have written to Y[ou] for I feel as tho we are under obligations to you for all the news we have from Haverhill and she can hear from father and mother just as well as tho it had been written to her. We are glad to hear she enjoyd her visit at Lowell & hope she will at Haverhill and mother say[s] she must write again and let her know how she is prospering.[58] If your mother is any worse write to us for we shall be glad to hear from her if we can not see her. Tell Jeremiah he must get ready to go to the West with me for I shall ceartainly go if I live and dont get married and I suppose you will think thare is no danger of that but I tell you thare has been many a biger fool then my self got maried so no more nor at this time.

M M Edwards

Letters of Jemima Edwards Sanborn and Ann Blake, 1843-1845

Nashville May the 14 1843

Dear Brother & Sister Bennett,[59]

I thought I would jest say a word to you if it is not quite so brite. Our famely is all in good health except myself. I have been q[u]ite out of health this spring but am much better now. The Doctor says I have the liver complaint. You will probely want to know the cause of our moveing here which are many. I will menshion afew of them. One of them is the hard times to get aliving off the farm for so large famely so we have devided our famely for this year. We have left Plummer and Luther to care on the farm with granmarm and aunt Polly.[60] The rest of us have moved here to Nashvill thinking the girles and Charles they would probely worke in the Mill. But we have had bad luck in giting them in only Jane has got in yet. Ann has the promis of going in the mill next week. Hannah is going to school. We are in hopes to take afew borders but have not got any yet. We live on canall street vary nere Indian head factory.[61] We heard from fathers folks last week. They were all well they had lately heard from Mary. She wrote she was well fat sausy and happy and had got a little girl the prittyest little

58. Mrs. Frisbee is Betsy Edwards Frisbie, Malenda's oldest sister, who was visiting her son in Lowell.
59. This letter is addressed to Richard and Ruth Edwards Bennett, Sabrina's parents. Jemima Sanborn is Ruth Bennett's sister and Sabrina's aunt.
60. Polly is Daniel Sanborn's unmarried older sister who lived with the family on the homestead in Bristol. Musgrove, *History of Bristol*, 2:367.
61. Canal Street in Nashua runs parallel to the Merrimack River right next to the mills of the Jackson Company. While the Sanborns had some initial difficulty finding work for their children, things improved over time. By 1845

babe you ever see. She sayd they ware agoing to move to Indinia [*sic*] in April. They wrote they had bought a farm there and ware agoing to farming. They did not write the name of the town so we dont know whar to derict a letter to her till we here from them. We have not herd from Brother Frisbye folks sence last winter. He was vary low and feeble then they did not expect he could live but alittle while. Brother [John] Bryant has got anew office he is postmaster and Depety Marshal of this state. David [Edwards] has moved to Nubury [Newbury] about nine miles from Bryants and taken afarm. I think Eliza would like to come down here and work in Mill. There is a grate many more trying to git in than can git in. It is quite apleasant place hear but it dont seeme much like home. It would seeme more like home if any of my folks lived here you know I never was weaned from fathers house before. It is rather a hard case but I suppose I must try and bare with it. You must come and see us as soon as you can it is only 20 miles. You can take the cars and come in a few minits.[62] I have some good news to tell you about father he became q[u]ite pious last fall. O Ruth it would have affected your heart to have seen our aged farther agoing fore[war]d to the anxious seats and bending the knee for prayers. He is vary particular to crave a blessing before eating. You know that is a grate undertaking for him. Thare was agrate many that professed to have meet with achaing [a change] last fall mostly old people. Sence we moved here we have hered that Luther and aunt Polly had experinced religion. I think Plummer will be vary much rejoiced to have so many of the familey join withe him in praising his maker. Sabryna I was vary sorrow to hear of your sickness I hope you are fast againeng your health. When you git well enough to ride abroad come and make us agood longe visit. I should have been glad if Ann could have gone to Haverhil and lernt the trade but she thinks she must try the mill aspell first for the want of clothes that is fit to wear. I think i shall not have to make any appology, only say that Daniel has gone to Brystol and you will not think strange of my bad spelling and interlineng. I am as lonesome as you can think here among all strangers. You must all come and see us as soon as you can. I must draw to acloas by subscrybing your loveing Sister

Jemima W Sanborn

---

the *Nashua Directory* recorded the following working family members and boarders: Malenda and James Edwards and Jane Sanborn, all working at the Jackson Company, and Ann Blake, employed as a dressmaker. Daniel and son Henry were noted also, but without occupations.

62. The cars mentioned here are trains of the Nashua and Lowell Railroad, completed in 1838.

Nashville May 14 1843

Dear Brother & Sister Bennett I thought I would just say a word to you if it is not quite so write our family is all in good health except my self I have been quite out of health this spring but am much better now the Doctor says I have the liver complaint, you will probably want to know the cause of our moveing here which are many I will menstion a few of them one of them is the hard times to get a liveing off the farm for so large family so we have devided our family for this year we have left Plummer and Luther to care on the farm with granmarm and aunt Polly the rest of us have moved here to Nashvill thinking the girls and boys they would probely worke in the Mill but we have had bad luck in giting them in only June has got in yet Ann has the promis of going in the mill next week Hannah is going to school we are in hopes to take of our bordens but have not got any yet we live on canall street vary near Indian head factory, we heard from fathers folks last week they were all well they had lately hair from Mary she wrote she was well but was syound happey and had got a fitt a girl the prittyest little babe you ever see she says they ware agoing to move to Indinia in April they write they had bought a farm there and ware agoing to farming they did not write the name of the town so we donot know whar to deriet a letter to them we have from them, we have not heard from Brother Tristye weeks sceven last winter he was vary low and feeble then they did n.t expect he live but a little while Brother Bryant has got an new office he is post master and I Depety Marshal of this sta'e

Jemima Sanborn letter, 1843.

[May 14 1843]

Dear Cousin,

It is with plasure I sit my self to write to you informing you of my good helth &c. I feel as well contented as could be expected. Concidering all things, I think it would be best for me to work in the mill a year and then I should be better prepared to learn a traid. I should like to have gone [to Haverhill] but our folks moving to Nashville I thought I should like to try the Mill and see how I like it. I think I shall like very mutch for I go in all moast every day to see Jane and have all moast stole the [letter torn]. I think I shall go in to work next weak. It is [letter torn] imposable for eny one to get in to the Mill they do not engage only half the help they did before they reduced the spead.[63] Ann and George Bryant was down this last winter.[64] George said he should come to Nashvill this summer he tho[u]ght in June and go to Haverhill. He was taken sick with his old complaint. His father came down and caried him home. His grandmother was down this spring she said he had got well so I think he will come. I think if I have good luck I shall go to Haverhill but do not wait for me. Come if you can conveniently. Farther is gon[e] to Bristol so we are very loanly. We received your letter and was very glad to hear from you.

You must excuse all bad mistakes as I am in a grate hurry. Give my love to all the good folks you know.

Ann M B[lake]

Nashville Sep 9th 1843

Dear cousin,

I had an opertunity to write to you by a girle by the name of Nancy Robings so thought I would improve it in the first plase. We got home safe and sound I was disapointed to think I could not go to St. Burwick but could not. Plummer was other ways engaged. We have received a letter from uncle Bryant he wrote the sad intelegents that cousin George is dead. He dide the 22 of Aug[ust] with that same diseas and on examination of the body after death it was found that a fleshy substance had grown in the canal of his hart. I commenced work with

63. It was a common practice on the part of management in the mills to reduce the speed of machinery, and thus reduce production, when inventories grew beyond customary levels. Since workers were paid according to their output this practice led to a significant cut in earnings.
64. Ann and George Bryant are cousins, children of John and Hannah Edwards Bryant. Musgrove, *History of Bristol*, 2:72-73.

Jackson Manufacturing Company, Nashua, New Hampshire, 1846.

a Miss Senter to work three months.[65] I like very mutch. You spoke of
my working with you. If you think it would be profitable for us boath I
will come the first of december. I shall lerne only the dressmaking.
Write to me if you would like to have me come & how mutch you
think we could make and if you have work plenty &c. I think our folks
will go back to Bristol the first of slaying but I shall not go if I can get
work to suit me. I should rather go to Haverhill then to stay here.
Uncle & Aunt Abrams are here to-day I cant write mutch more fore
want [of] paper. Mother thinks I habe better go back to Bristol but I do
not think so if I can do eny thing to my proffit eny where. Write soon
& all the particulars. As fore paper you will see we have but a bit.
Excuse all mistakes and remember your friend

An[n] M Blake

[Bristol, N.H.] September the 2 [1845]

Brothers & Sisters,[66]

What shall I give for an excuse for not writing to you before this
time, in the first place I had rather be whip[p]ed than to write a letter
and then in the next place I have been gone from home cince you went
away Betsey. I went down and stayed with Sally [Edwards Heath] most
a week after her boy was born. She has a smart fat boy. Cince then
Ann & I have been to Gilmanto[n] found most of the people well. Cap
Norris is as crazy as lave dont do any work at all. Cap Chase was jest
gone with the dropsey. It is a generl time of helth here now. My health
is about the same that it was when you left the rest all in usu[a]l
health. Father and Mother health is as good as can be expetd for old
people. Father was rather slim when he first begun his haying but after
a few days he became quite smart and worked all the time through
haying and repeing. Mr. D is gone up to Mr. Clarks to work again and
Horrice Persons is to work for farther now. Melinda [Edwards] had a
letter from Mary [Edwards Colby] a few weeks ago. She rote they ware
all well and prospering finely. She sayed she plucked amay flower in
the month of May the prittest you ever see in your life. It was she
sayed a white flower with blue eyes. She talks calling its name Ellen
James for his brother and hern.[67] Mary sayes they built a framed house

65. Numerous Senters resided in Nashua at this time according to city direc-
tories, although none were recorded as dressmakers or milliners.
66. This letter is addressed to two couples, Richard and Ruth Bennett, and
Timothy and Betsey Frisbie, both of whom resided in Haverhill at this date.
Ruth and Betsey are sisters of Jemima Edwards Sanborn.
67. This "may flower" is Mary Colby's son, Allen James.

with four rooms and then in addition to that they have a large brick house and a[l]most all paid for. They now keep a grocery and are agoing to keeping tavern soon. She think they shall come here to see the folks in the course of two or three years if father and Mother lives. Well Sabrina how are you aprospering now? Are you as near the eave of gitting married as your cousin Ann Briant? I understand she is soon to have the knot tied.[68] I am agood mind to tell you how near we have come of haveing an invite to the wedding. She has sent down to Hebron for Emeline Berry and that comming vary nere. Oscor F was there about aweek ago. He sayed she was to be married in about two week then and was agoing to start for the south was not acomming this way to show her man. S[abrina] I saw a gentleman and lady from your town a week ago last sunday to our meeting. His name was Carlton his wife works in the shop with Mrs. Blaisding. They went from Hill. Our girles are at home now but think of going into the mill here at Bristol in about two or three week. Plummer and wife have gone down to her fathers and to the salt watter and Luther and aunt Polly they have gone over a week.[69] P & S[arah] expects to bee gone three weeks. Wee look for l[uther and] Polly home tomorrow. Ruth, I am sorrow to here your health is so poor. I was in hopes we should see you up here this fall but am afraid we shall not but keep up good courage for that is one half of the battle. But I am apoor hand to give advice my health is so poor I feel quite discoureged a good part of the time but that dont do me aney good I find. Betsey how is your health now and how are you injoying your self now? And what are you thinking of doing this winter? Are you agoing to stay there or what are you agoing to do? Any way give my love to all inquiring friends and expect [sic] alarge shere your selves.

Jemima W. Sandom [Sanborn]

Mrs. Frisbie

You know we heared that aunt [Malenda] Edwards was now married. It is not so nor she does not talk of it nor father Blak[e] neither but is going to be soon I suppose to the old maid that keeps his house. We herd from David's folks a while ago. They ware all weel then. We look for Bryants folks down this fall as soon as Ann is gone [i.e., married]. S, why cant you and the boys come up this fall while your aunt Betsey is there with your mother? There I believe I have rote all the news I can think of. Only Daniel is up to fathers ahelping him

68. Ann Bryant married Gardner Elliott, Sept. 23, 1845. Musgrove, *History of Bristol*, 2:72.

69. Plummer married Sarah F. Dearborn in May 1844. Musgrove, *History of Bristol*, 2:369.

brake up so that he cant put aword in this time. You must all come up as soon as you can and be shure and write as soon as you git this and write all the news you can think of. What a sad thing it was to have cousin William taken away so sudden and then his wife to follow him so soon. How quick the famely was broke up so we see when we are in the midst of life we are in death. I must draw to aclose for I am so ful of blunders can but jist read my own writing and I am fraid you cant read it at all

O, Mrs Betsey, Mr Dustain wants to git him a wife he says he should like one about 18 so I am afraide there wont be a chance for yourn.

Jemima W Sandborn

Thursday September the 4

Lowell shopping district, 1856, shortly after Mary Paul worked in Lowell.

THREE

Mary Paul Letters

MARY PAUL, the daughter of Bela and Mary Briggs Paul, grew up in Woodstock and Barnard, in northern Vermont. The third of four children, Mary led a migratory life from the age of fifteen until her marriage at twenty-seven. We have a clear record of these years because Mary proved a steady correspondent and her father saved twenty-five of her letters that cover the seventeen-year period between her departure from home in 1845 and the last letter in this collection, dated April 1862. The correspondence offers a rare view into the work and family experiences of one woman whose life was touched by mill employment.[1]

Judging by the letters, Mary Paul was a restless spirit. She moved around from place to place and job to job in these years. The letters open with Mary employed as a domestic with a farming family in Bridgewater, just a few miles from her family home in Barnard. Difficulties there led to her departure and her entrance into the textile mills of Lowell, Massachusetts. She labored off and on in Lowell for the next four years, but returned home to Claremont, New Hampshire, where her widowed father resided in 1850.[2] Two years later her letters show her living in Brattleboro, Vermont making coats in a partnership with another woman. After two years there, she was off to Redbank, New Jersey, where she resided in a utopian agricultural community for a year with friends she had met in Lowell.[3] After that undertaking collapsed, she returned to New Hampshire for a stint as a housekeeper. Finally, in 1857, after twelve years of supporting herself away from home, Mary Paul married

1. Paul Family Genealogy and Mary Paul Letters, Vermont Historical Society, Montpelier, Vt.; hereafter cited as VHS. See also letters from Mary's brother, William Paul.
2. Bela Paul, sixty, and Mary Paul, twenty-one, are recorded in the 1850 Census in dwelling 533 in Claremont, N.H.
3. The North American Phalanx, founded by American followers of Charles Fourier, was the largest and most successful of the phalanxes, with more than a hundred members when Mary Paul joined in 1855.

Isaac Guild, the son of her former Lowell boardinghouse keeper. The new couple moved to Lynn, Massachusetts, where Isaac found employment in a marble works. Mary Paul Guild bore two children over the next five years, and domestic concerns dominate her correspondence with her father. Bela Paul by this date had moved to Windsor, Vermont, and lived with a married son. He died in 1863, at the age of seventy-nine, an event that may well account for the ending point of this collection.[4]

Mary Paul's letters offer repeated examples of the importance of economic independence and continued family ties for mill workers. Although economic motives are paramount in Mary Paul's initial decision to enter the mills, it is important to note that she has individual economic gain in mind. Hers is not a family decision—though she seeks her father's approval—to send a daughter to work. She expected to do better for herself in Lowell than she could in rural Vermont. While in Lowell she supported herself quite adequately. In her first eleven months in the mills she earned $128, an average of about $2.70 a week. With room and board in company housing set at $1.25 each week, she would have had a margin to buy clothes, attend church and lectures, and still save stagecoach fare to permit her to return home.[5]

Her father was a widower in these years and was not in the best of health. Mary offers him occasional bits of advice and clearly would have liked to have taken better care of him in his old age. As she wrote in 1853: "I hope sometime to be able to do something for you and sometimes feel ashamed that I have not before this." And although Bela Paul does visit his daughter briefly when she is married and living in Lynn, Mary continues to live apart from her father. Despite some evident guilt, personal economic need proves more pressing than her sense of familial obligation. As she explains in one letter: "[I] must work where I can get more pay."[6]

Mary Paul's strong ties to her family are evident throughout her correspondence. Her letters are punctuated with questions about family members and expressions of concern for them. When Mary first went to Lowell she wrote of her disappointment that her father and brothers had not come down to see her off. She suggested that her family move to Lowell, indicating that her brothers could find employment in the mills.

4. For marriage and birth records see Massachusetts Bureau of Vital Records, vol. 109, p. 147; Irving Tracy Guild, December 30, 1860, vol. 132, p. 268; Sidney Pratt Guild, August 31, 1862, vol. 150, p. 230.
5. Lawrence Manufacturing Company Payrolls, Vol. GB-8, Manuscript Division, Baker Library, Harvard Business School.
6. Mary Paul to Bela Paul, Nov. 27, Dec. 18, 1853.

There was evidently a lively family correspondence, particularly with brother William who lived in Tennessee at this time. Other relatives figure in the letters, Aunt and Uncle Miller in Woodstock, and Uncle Jerry in Claremont, New Hampshire, in particular. It is evident that although Mary Paul left home to work by herself in Lowell, she was by no means distant from her family.

These letters strikingly reveal a gap between the actual experiences of women in this period and contemporary ideals concerning "woman's sphere." These years saw the rise of what one historian has termed the "Cult of True Womanhood," that body of prescriptive literature which defined women in terms of their roles as wives and mothers.[7] Women were viewed as particularly suited for domestic pursuits; their influence in the world was felt primarily within the familial circle. Their position in society was characterized by submission and dependence, first as daughters in the parental home, and later as wives under their husbands' sway. In contrast to this ideal, Mary Paul lived away from family twelve years before her marriage, and there were undoubtedly many women like her.[8] In Mary Paul's letters we see evidence of the increased economic and social independence enjoyed by many single women even in the face of the dominant ideology. They suggest the importance for historians of constantly testing broad ideals against the realities of the concrete attitudes and behavior evident in the everyday lives of ordinary men and women.

Bridgewater [Vt.] July 25th 1845[9]

Dear Father

Mr. Angell received your letter on the 22nd And I supposed would do something about my staying, but he has not.[10] And so I thought I would write to you & have you come over yourself. I did not leave

---

7. Barbara Welter, "The Cult of True Womanhood," *American Quarterly*, (1966) 18:151-74.

8. For the 175 women workers from the Hamilton Company in Lowell discussed in the introduction the mean length of time between beginning mill employment and marriage was almost eight years.

9. This letter, like the next five, is addressed to Bela Paul in Barnard, Vt. Bela is a widower at this time, his wife having died four years earlier. Mary is fifteen years old and is living in Bridgewater, a farming town about fourteen miles from Barnard. Paul Family Genealogy, VHS.

10. The Angells are probably Colburn and Clarissa Angell recorded in dwelling 103 in the 1850 Census of Bridgewater.

uncle Millers until Sunday morning. Aunt Sarah was quite sick [and I] have not heard from her since. Mrs. A did not speak to me after I got home till after supper but she has done remarkably well since your letter came. I suppose Mr A wants I should stay but I do not want to. I did not see as anything was going to be done and for that reason I write. I suppose Aunt Nancy expects me every day but she will not see me till you come.[11]

I want you to start as soon as you receive this.

Yours,

Mary

[Woodstock, Vt.] Saturday Sept. 13th 1845[12]

Dear Father

I received your letter this afternoon by Wm Griffith. You wished me to write if I had seen Mr. Angell. I have neither written to him nor seen him nor has he written to me. I began to write but I could not write what I wanted to. I think if I could see him I could convince him of his error if he would let me talk. I am very glad you sent my shoes. They fit very well indeed they [are] large enough.

I want you to consent to let me go to Lowell if you can. I think it would be much better for me than to stay about here. I could earn more to begin with than I can any where about here. I am in need of clothes which I cannot get if I stay about here and for that reason I want to go to Lowell or some other place. We all think if I could go with some steady girl that I might do well. I want you to think of it and make up your mind. Mercy Jane Griffith is going to start in four or five weeks. Aunt Miller and Aunt Sarah think it would be a good chance for me to go if you would consent—which I want you to do if possible. I want to see you and talk with you about it.

Aunt Sarah gains slowly.

Mary

Bela Paul

11. Uncle Miller and Aunt Nancy are Nathaniel and Nancy Paul Miller who resided in nearby Woodstock. Aunt Sarah is Sarah Paul, an unmarried younger sister of Bela Paul. Paul Family Genealogy, VHS; 1850 Census of Woodstock, dwelling 372.

12. The postmark of this letter and its contents indicate that Mary has left the Angells and come to Woodstock, about eight miles from Barnard, where she is staying with the Millers.

Woodstock Nov 8 1845

Dear Father

As you wanted me to let you know when I am going to start for
Lowell, I improve this opportunity to write you. Next Thursday the
13th of this month is the day set or the Thursday afternoon. I should
like to have you come down. If you come bring Henry if you can for I
should like to see him before I go. Julius has got the money for me.[13]

Yours Mary

Lowell Nov 20th 1845

Dear Father

An opportunity now presents itself which I improve in writing to
you. I started for this place at the time I talked of which was Thursday.
I left Whitneys at nine o'clock stopped at Windsor at 12 and staid till 3
and started again. Did not stop again for any length of time till we
arrived at Lowell. Went to a boarding house and staid until Monday
night. On Saturday after I got here Luthera Griffith went round with
me to find a place but we were unsuccessful. On Monday we started
again and were more successful. We found a place in a spinning room
and the next morning I went to work. I like very well have 50 cts first
payment increasing every payment as I get along in work have a first
rate overseer and a very good boarding place. I work on the Lawrence
Corporation. Mill is No 2 spinning room.[14] I was very sorry that you
did not come to see me start. I wanted to see you and Henry but I
suppose that you were otherways engaged. I hoped to see Julius but
did not much expect to for I s[up]posed he was engaged in other
matters. He got six dollars for me which I was very glad of. It cost me
$3.25 to come. Stage fare was $3.00 and lodging at Windsor, 25 cts.
Had to pay only 25 cts for board for 9 days after I got here before I
went into the mill. Had 2.50 left with which I got a bonnet and some
other small articles. Tell Harriet Burbank to send me paper. Tell her I
shall send her one as soon as possible. You must write as soon as you

13. The references here are to two of Mary's brothers, Henry and Julius, both
apparently living with their father at this time. Henry was thirteen and Julius
twenty-seven. Paul Family Genealogy, VHS.
14. Surviving payrolls reveal that Mary Paul earned $0.30 per day in her first
month in the mill, making $1.80 per week, or $0.55 above the cost of room
and board. Lawrence Manufacturing Company Records, Vol. GB-8, Spinning
Room No. 2, Nov. 20, 1845.

Lawrence Company boardinghouses.

receive this. Tell Henry I should like to hear from him. If you hear anything from William write for I want to know what he is doing.[15] I shall write to Uncle Millers folks the first opportunity. Aunt Nancy presented me with a new alpacca dress before I came away from there which I was very glad of. I think of staying here a year certain, if not more. I wish that you and Henry would come down here. I think that you might do well. I guess that Henry could get into the mill and I think that Julius might get in too. Tell all friends that I should like to hear from them.

excuse bad writing and mistakes
This from your own daughter
Mary

P.S. Be sure and direct to No. 15 Lawrence Corporation.
Bela Paul

Mary S Paul

Lowell Dec 21st 1845

Dear Father

I received your letter on Thursday the 14th with much pleasure. I am well which is one comfort. My life and health are spared while others are cut off. Last Thursday one girl fell down and broke her neck which caused instant death. She was going in or coming out of the mill and slipped down it being very icy. The same day a man was killed by the cars.[16] Another had nearly all of his ribs broken. Another was nearly killed by falling down and having a bale of cotton fall on him. Last Tuesday we were paid. In all I had six dollars and sixty cents paid $4.68 for board. With the rest I got me a pair of rubbers and a pair of 50.cts shoes. Next payment I am to have a dollar a week beside my board.[17] We have not had much snow the deepest being not more than 4 inches. It has been very warm for winter. Perhaps you would like

15. There are repeated references to William, a third brother who lived and married in Tennessee during these years. Paul Family Genealogy; Letters of William Paul, VHS.

16. These were probably the cars of the Boston and Lowell Railroad. Each firm had railroad siding running right up to the mills to facilitate transport of raw cotton and finished cloth.

17. In fact, Mary earned only $2.04 per week during the payroll period which ended January 10, 1846, making $0.79 above the cost of room and board. She worked as a doffer removing full bobbins of yarn from the spinning frames and replacing them with empty ones. The work called for speed and dexterity, but it was intermittent, requiring only about fifteen minutes of activity out of each hour. Doffers were almost always children, usually sons or daughters of boardinghouse keepers or skilled workers.

something about our regulations about going in and coming out of the mill. At 5 o'clock in the morning the bell rings for the folks to get up and get breakfast. At half past six it rings for the girls to get up and at seven they are called into the mill. At half past 12 we have dinner are called back again at one and stay till half past seven.[18] I get along very well with my work. I can doff as fast as any girl in our room. I think I shall have frames before long. The usual time allowed for learning is six months but I think I shall have frames before I have been in three as I get along so fast. I think that the factory is the best place for me and if any girl wants employment I advise them to come to Lowell. Tell Harriet that though she does not hear from me she is not forgotten. I have little time to devote to writing that I cannot write all I want to. There are half a dozen letters which I ought to write to day but I have not time. Tell Harriet I send my love to her and all of the girls. Give my love to Mrs. Clement. Tell Henry this will answer for him and you too for this time.

This from
Mary S Paul

Bela Paul
Henry S Paul

Lowell April 12th 1846

Dear Father

I received your letter with much pleasure but was sorry to hear that you had been lame. I had waited for a long time to hear from you but no letter came so last Sunday I thought I would write again which I did and was going to send it to the [post] office Monday but at noon I received a letter from William and so I did not send it at all. Last Friday I received a letter from you. You wanted to know what I am doing. I am at work in a spinning room and tending four sides of warp which is one girls work. The overseer tells me that he never had a girl get along better than I do and that he will do the best he can by me. I stand it well, though they tell me that I am growing very poor. I was paid nine shillings a week last payment and am to have more this one though we have been out considerable for backwater which will take off a good deal.[19] The Agent promises to pay us nearly as much as we

18. Mary is outlining the winter schedule, when operatives took breakfast before beginning work. In the summer months, as the next letter indicates, work began at 5:00 A.M. and operatives had short breaks for breakfast and dinner during the working day.

19. Mary tended four sides of warp spinning frames, each with 128 spindles,

should have made but I do not think that he will. The payment was up last night and we are to be paid this week.[20] I have a very good boarding place have enough to eat and that which is good enough. The girls are all kind and obliging. The girls that I room with are all from Vermont and good girls too. Now I will tell you about our rules at the boarding house. We have none in particular except that we have to go to bed about 10. o'clock. At half past 4 in the morning the bell rings for us to get up and at five for us to go into the mill. At seven we are called out to breakfast are allowed half an hour between bells and the same at noon till the first of May when we have three quarters [of an hour] till the first of September. We have dinner at half past 12 and supper at seven. If Julius should go to Boston tell him to come this way and see me. He must come to the Lawrence Counting room and call for me. He can ask some one to show him where the Lawrence is. I hope he will not fail to go. I forgot to tell you that I have not seen a particle of snow for six weeks and it is settled going we have had a very mild winter and but little snow. I saw Ann Hersey last Sunday. I did not know her till she told me who she was. I see the Griffith girls often. I received a letter from a girl in Bridgewater in which she told me that Mrs Angell had heard some way that I could not get work and that she was much pleased and said that I was so bad that no one would have me. I believe I have written all so I will close for I have a letter to write to William this afternoon.

Yours affectionately
Mary S Paul

Mr. Bela Paul

P.S. Give my love to all that enquire for me and tell them to write me a long long letter. Tell Harriet I shall send her a paper.

-----

the normal complement for spinners in these years. She quoted her wages in English currency, though she was undoubtedly paid American money, nine shillings being equal to $1.50. As in the earlier cases, Mary is referring to her wages exclusive of room and board charges. "Backwater," mentioned here, was a common problem in the spring, when heavy run-off due to rains and melting snow led to high water levels, causing water to back up and block the waterwheel. Mills often had to cease operations for several days at a time. The April payroll at the Lawrence Comapany indicates that Mary worked only fifteen of the normal twenty-four days in the payroll period.

20. It was standard practice to post on a blackboard in each room of the mills the production and the earnings of each worker several days before the monthly payday, to enable operatives to see what they would be paid and to complain if the posted production figures did not agree with their own records of the work.

Lowell Nov 5th 1848[21]

Dear Father

Doubtless you have been looking for a letter from me all the week past. I would have written but wished to find whether I should be able to stand it—to do the work that I am now doing. I was unable to get my old place in the cloth room on the Suffolk or on any other corporation. I next tried the dressrooms on the Lawrence Cor[poration], but did not succe[e]d in getting a place. I almost concluded to give up and go back to Claremont, but thought I would try once more. So I went to my old overseer on the Tremont Cor. I had no idea that he would want one, but he *did*, and I went to work last Tuesday— warping—the same work I used to do.[22]

It is *very* hard indeed and sometimes I think I shall not be able to endure it. I never worked so hard in my life but perhaps I shall get used to it. I shall try hard to do so for there is no other work that I can do unless I spin and that I shall not undertake on any account. I presume you have heard before this that the wages are to be reduced on the 20th of this month. It is *true* and there seems to be a good deal of excitement on the subject but I can not tell what will be the consequence.[23] The companies pretend they are losing immense sums every *day* and therefore they are obliged to lessen the wages, but this seems perfectly absurd to me for they are constantly making *repairs* and it seems to me that this would not be if there were really any danger of their being obliged to *stop* the mills.

It is very difficult for any one to get into the mill on any corporation. All seem to be very full of help. I expect to be paid about two dollars a week but it will be dearly earned.[24] I cannot tell how it is but never

21. Mary Paul has left and returned to Lowell since her previous letter. She remained at the Lawrence Company until the end of October 1846. Lawrence Company payrolls, Vol. GB-8. This letter is addressed to Claremont, N.H., where her father has recently moved.

22. The "dressroom" mentioned here would be a dressing room in the mill where warp yarn was prepared for the weaving process. Generally speaking, more experienced women worked in the dressing room, wages and conditions of work being considerably better there than in the carding and spinning rooms.

23. Wages were reduced in all of the Lowell mills in November 1848. See Henry Hall to John Aiken, September 4, 1848, Lawrence Company Records; Henry Hall to John Wright, September 4, 1848, Vol. FB-3, Tremont-Suffolk Mills Records, Baker Library, Harvard Business School.

24. This wage figure, $2.00 per week, again refers to earnings exclusive of charges for room and board. The overall figure of $3.25 weekly was extremely low for warpers, usually among the best-paid women workers in the mills. Thomas Dublin, *Women at Work: The Transformation of Work and Community in Lowell, Massachusetts, 1826-1860* (New York: Columbia University Press, 1979), pp. 66, 159.

since I have worked in the mill have I been so very tired as I have for the last week but it may be owing to the long rest I have had for the last six months. I have not told you that I do not board on the Lawrence. The reason of this is because I wish to be nearer the mill and I do not wish to pay the extra $.12-1/2 per week (I should not be obliged to do it if I boarded at 15) and I know that they are not able to give it me. Beside this I am so near I can go and see them as often as I wish. So considering all things I think I have done the best I could. I do not like here very well and am very sure I never shall as well as at Mother Guilds. I can now realize how very kind the whole family have ever been to me. It seems like going *home* when I go there which is every day.[25] But now I see I have not told you yet where I do board. It is at No. 5 Tremont Corporation. Please enlighten all who wish for information. There is one thing which I forgot to bring with me and which I want very much. That is my *rubbers*. They hang in the back room at uncle Jerrys.[26] If Olive comes down here I presume you can send them by her, but if you should not have the opportunity to send them do not trouble yourself about them. There is another thing I wish to mention—about my fare down here. If you paid it all the way as I understand you did there is something wrong about it. When we stopped at Concord to take the cars, I went to the ticket office to get a ticket which I knew I should be obliged to have. When I called for it I told the man that my fare to Lowell was paid all the way and I wanted a ticket to Lowell. He told me if this was the case the Stagedriver would get the ticket for me and I supposed of course he would. But he did *not*, and when the ticket master called for my ticket in the *cars*, I was obliged to give him a dollar. Sometimes I have thought that the fare might *not* have been paid beside farther than Concord. If this is the case all is right. But if it is not, then I have paid a dollar too much and gained the character of trying to cheat the company out of my fare, for the man thought I was lying to him. I suppose I want to know how it is and wish it could be settled for I do not like that *any* one should think *me* capable of such a thing, even though that person be an utter stranger. But enough of this. The Whigs of Lowell had a great time on

25. "Mother Guild" refers to Mrs. Betsey Guild who, with her husband, kept a boardinghouse at 15 Lawrence Company at least between 1847 and 1853. Mary Paul did get to know and like the "whole family," as she indicates, for in 1857 she married a son, Isaac, and settled in Lynn. Lowell *Directory*, 1847-1853; Massachusetts Bureau of Vital Records, vol. 109, p. 147.

26. Jerry refers to Jeremiah Paul who lived with his wife, Betsey, and two young children in Claremont, N.H. "Little Lois," mentioned at the end of this letter, was their two-year-old daughter. 1850 Census of Claremont, dwelling 407.

the night of the 3rd. They had an immense procession of men on foot bearing *torches* and *banners* got up for the occasion. The houses were illuminated (Whigs houses) and by the way I should think the whole of *Lowell* were Whigs. I went out to see the illuminations and they did truly look splendid. The Merrimack house was illuminated from attic to cellar.[27] Every pane of glass in the house had a half candle to it and there were many others lighted in the same way. One entire block on the Merrimack Cor[poration] with the exception of one tenement which doubtless was occupied by a free soiler who would not illuminate on any account whatever.[28]

(Monday Eve) I have been to work today and think I shall manage to get along with the work. I am not so tired as I was last week. I have not yet found out what wages I shall get but presume they will be about $2.00 per week exclusive of board. I think of nothing further to write excepting I wish you to prevail on *Henry* to write to me, also tell *Olive* to write and *Eveline* when she comes.[29]

Give my love to uncle Jerry and aunt Betsey and tell little Lois that "Cousin Carra" thanks her very much for the *apple* she sent her. Her health is about the same that it was when she was at Claremont. No one has much hope of her ever being any better.

Write soon. Yours affectionately
Mary S Paul

Mr. Bela Paul
P.S. Do not forget to direct to No. 5 Tremont Cor and tell all others to do the same.

═══════════

Lowell July 1st 1849

Dear Father

I received your letter dated the 25. of June on Wednesday the 27. and would have answered immediately but had not time. I was very glad to get the letters from William. I had almost given up the hope of

---

27. The Merrimack House was the leading hotel in Lowell and usually housed distinguished visitors and millowners when they came to town. The date of the illumination, November 3, suggests it was part of election day festivities.

28. The Free Soil Party was a third party opposed to the extension of slavery into the territories acquired in the recent Mexican War. Former President Martin Van Buren ran on its ticket in 1848.

29. Eveline here is Eveline Sperry Paul, the wife of Seth Paul, another younger brother of Bela. Subsequent letters also refer to their oldest son, Seth Jr. Paul Family Genealogy, VHS; 1850 Census for Claremont, dwelling 135.

hearing from him and had commenced a letter to him when yours came in which *his* [was] enclosed. I will give you his words in regard to his health &c: "As for my own health, it has been generally very good. Though for the last few days I have been quite unwell and was confined to my *bed* for a day or two. I feel quite unsure at this time." And of the Cholera he says, "It has broken out fearfully within a few days on the 10th inst. (June) there were 10 deaths from it, on the 11th 25, and I have not heard the report for yesterday (the 12th)."[30]

He is often in the Prison and will probably remain there until a better situation offers. He says "tell Henry I will write to him without fail before long."

My health has been pretty good though I have been obliged to be out of the mill four days. I thought *then* that it would be impossible for me to work through the hot weather. But since I think I shall manage to get through after a fashion. I do not know what wages I am to have as I have not yet been paid but I shall not expect *much*, as I have not been able to *do* much, although I have worked very hard.[31] I shall send a letter with this to Eveline so that you can give it to her when you see her. Give my love to Henry and tell him I will write him as soon as I can and tell him to write and not *wait* for *me*.

Yours affectionately
Mary S Paul

Brattleboro [Vermont] Nov. 7th 1852[32]

Dear father

I received a letter from Henry last night inclosing yours from William. He (Henry) said you wished me to send it back to you as you were going to send it to Julius. I send it therefore with this. His letter

---

30. A cholera epidemic swept through American cities in the first half of 1849. William Paul was an officer in the Tennessee Penitentiary in Nashville at this date. "The Affairs of William P. Paul," typescript, VHS; Charles E. Rosenberg, *The Cholera Years: The United States in 1832, 1849 and 1866* (Chicago: University of Chicago Press, 1962).

31. The fact that Mary Paul does not know what her wages will be suggests that she has recently returned to the mills after a period of absence. Since earnings were based on piece wage rates, it always took a new worker a month or two to determine exactly how much she could expect to earn.

32. The previous letter is the last one Mary wrote from Lowell. In 1850 she was back in Claremont living with her father, Bela, in the dwelling of William and Olive Kimball. There have been numerous references in the letters to Olive, who may have been a cousin. This letter is sent from Brattleboro, Vt., where Mary is working as a seamstress.

MERRIMACK HOUSE,

Pendleton's Lithography, Boston

Merrimack House, 1835.

contained also the news of the death of Frank Sperry. I think the
family must take it rather hard. I wrote to William last Sunday and
directed the letter to Nashville, Tenn. but I do not know as I ought to
have done so as his letter is mailed at Jasper, Tenn. if I read rightly.
When you write to him I wish you would tell him that I have written
and directed to Nashville. I wrote to Julius also last Sunday. I presume
he will be surprised to get a letter from me still I thought he might like
the idea after all. I do not know as I have any news to write. I am well
and doing pretty well. Abby and I have hired a stove for our room and
bought half a cord of wood so we are quite comfortable these cold
damp days and evenings. Have you had your rooms partitioned off
yet? If not I hope you will before it comes to be much colder. We had
quite a storm here last night. The wind blew so hard that we who sleep
in the upper part of the house began to fear the roof would blow off.
The house is four stories high. It makes me think of the house Adams
told about, that was 500 ft. long 700 ft. high and 2 ft. wide. It is getting
dark, so I must close hoping you will write soon. Love to Uncle Jerry
and family.

> Yours affectionately
> Mary S Paul

> Brattleboro Nov. 6th 1853

Dear Father

    I dont know but that you are waiting for me to write to you, as I
have been waiting for you. I have no news of any importance to write
that I know of, excepting that I received a letter from William a few
days since. He was well, and doing about the same as when he wrote
you. Is employed by the same firm as when he wrote, not married yet
but expecting to be sometime.[33] He said he would write you soon. It is
very cold here today. The ground was covered with snow this morning,
but there is little to be seen now excepting on the hills in the distance.
I am sorry that winter is so near us. I dread the cold. Abby is at
Guilford today. One of her brother's wives is very sick there. I have
not heard from Henry for some time. I wish Julius would write to me. I
sent him a paper last week. I wonder if he got it. Last night I saw a
paper containing Cousin Louise Briggs marriage. It was a paper edited
by her husband, a Mr. Stebbins of Michigan town of Adrian. I saw the

33. William Paul married Lucy McIntosh in March 1854 and they had two
children before she died in 1857. Paul Family Genealogy, VHS.

same notice in a Claremont paper a few days before. It was very unexpected to me, and I think it must have been sudden to her. She has an uncle here by the name of Woods, and Mrs. Woods gave me the information. Mr. Woods is in company with Mr. Carpenter in the Melodeon business. Mr. Carpenter is the man I am boarding with. How is Olive nowadays? Is she well and strong again? Are Uncle Jerry's family well? Give my love to them when you see them. I am getting along in the shop as usual. Have been making coats for a few weeks. I like it pretty well and am hoping to do better than on smaller jobs. I have plenty to do all the time. Write very soon for I am anxious to hear from you.

Yours affectionately

Mary S Paul

Brattleboro Nov. 27, 1853

Dear father

I think I will write you a few words tonight as you may be wishing to hear from me. Your letter of Nov. 13th tells me that you have been lame. I was sorry to hear it though I expected as much from your not writing before. It troubles me very much, the thought of your being lame so much and alone too. If there were any way that I could make it expedient I would go back to Claremont myself and I sometimes think I ought to do so but the chance for one there is so *small*, and I can do so much better elsewhere that I have thought it was really better for me to be somewhere else. But the thought of you always makes me wish to be where I can see you oftener. I feel anxious about Julius. I really wish that he might find steady employment at some good business. I am so sorry that he and Uncle Seth could not manage to agree. I wonder if he ever got the paper I sent him several weeks ago?

I have a plan for myself which I am going to lay before you and see what you think of it. When I was at Manchester last spring my friend Carrie and her husband were talking of going to New Jersey to live and proposed that I should go with them. They have decided to go and are thinking of going in a few weeks, maybe as soon as Jan. though they may not go until April or May. I have been thinking of it all summer, and have told them that I will go if you do not object. I can hardly get *my own* consent to go any farther away from you, though I know that in reality a few miles cannot make much difference. The name of the town is Atlantic is about 40 miles from New York City.

The people among whom they are going are Associationists.[34] The name will give you something of an idea of their principles. There [are] about 125 persons in all that live there, and the association is called the "North American Phalanx." I presume that you may have heard of it. You have if you read the "Tribune." The editor Mr "Greely"[35] is an Associationist and a shareholder in the "Phalanx," but he does not live there. The advantage that will arise from my going there will be that I can get better pay without working as hard as at any other place. The price for work there being 9 cts an hour, and the number of hours for a days work, *ten* besides I should not be confined to one kind of work but could do almost anything, could have the *privilege* of doing anything that is done there—*Housework* if I choose and that without degrading myself, which is more than I could do anywhere else. That is, in the opinion of most people, a very foolish and wrong idea by the way, but one that has so much weight with girls, that they would live on 25 cts per week at sewing, or school teaching rather than work at housework. I would do it myself although I think it foolish. This all comes from the way servants are *treated*, and I cannot see why girls can be blamed after all, for not wishing to "work out" as it is called. At the "Phalanx" it is different. *All* work there, and all are paid alike. Both men and women have the *same pay* for the *same* work. There is no such word as *aristocracy* there unless there is *real* (not pretended) superiority, *that* will make itself *felt*, if *not acknowledged, everywhere.* The *members* can live as *cheaply* as they choose as they pay only for what they *eat*, and no *profit* on that, most of the provision being raised on the grounds. One can join them with or without funds, and can leave at any time they choose. Frank has been there this Fall and was very much pleased with what he saw there and thought that it would be the best thing for Carrie and me to do with ourselves. A woman gets much better pay there than elsewhere, but it is not so with a man, though he is not *meanly* paid by any means. There is more equality in such things according to the *work* not the sex. You know that men often get more than double the pay for doing the same work that women do. Carrie and Frank are both Associationists and have been almost ever since I knew them, and I am acquainted with many others who are and their

34. The Associationists were utopian reformers, followers of Charles Fourier. They established model communities, or phalanxes, throughout the Northeast and Midwest in the 1840s and 1850s.
35. Horace Greeley, editor of the New York *Tribune*, was an early supporter of Association, attended numerous national conventions of the movement, and gave it support in the pages of his newspaper.

principles are just what I would like to see carried into practice and they *are* as far as means will allow at the Phalanx. Another advantage from living there is this, the members can have privileges of *Education* free of expense to themselves alone, the extent of this Education must of course depend on the *means* of the society. If I could see you I could give you a better idea. That I can possibly do by writing, but you will know something by this, enough to form an opinion perhaps and I wish you to let me know what you think of my plans. If you have any real objection or if you would rather I would not go so far away, let me know and I will cheerfully give up the idea of going. I hope sometime to be able to do something for you sometime and sometimes feel ashamed that I have not before this. I am not one of the *smart* kind, and never had a passion for laying up money, probably never shall have, can find ways enough to spend it though (but I do not wish to be extravagant). Putting all these things together I think explains the reason that I do not "lay up" anything. One thing more, I have never had very good pay. I am getting along slowly on coats, and shall do better as I get used to the business. I can work at my trade if I wish at the Phalanx. How are Uncle Jerry's family? Give my love to them and Julius when you see him. I hope you will write me very soon as I shall be very anxious to know your mind and I wish to let Carrie know. If you should think it best for me to go I shall visit C[laremont] in the course of a few weeks that is if we go in Jan. If not till April I shall not probably come to C[laremont] until about that time. I have written you quite a long letter and it is not very plain. I am afraid you will never be able to read it. I ought to have written more plainly but I am in something of a hurry and must offer that as my excuse. Write immediately, please.

Affectionately yours
Mary S Paul

Brattleboro Dec. 18, 1853

Dear Father

I am *very* tired tonight but I suppose you are anxious to hear from me so I will write a letter. I was glad to find from your letter that you approve my plans in regard to going to New Jersey. I have not heard anything definite about my going since I wrote you. I am hoping to know *something* very soon and then I will let you know. I suppose Henry will be here on his way to Claremont soon. He will tell you when you see him what the Lowell folks think of these things also his own opinion I suppose.[36] The thing seems to meet with general approbation and I still think it the very best thing I can do. I may not go till Spring, may not go at all. They may refuse us for our want of money to invest. Still if they do, I think we shall try to go *sometime*.

Last week I received a letter from William. He was well and sent love to you, was expecting a letter from you. You spoke in your letter of your wish to have a home for us all. I *wish* it too dear father, but not on my own account. I find comfortable homes almost everywhere and have no reason to complain of my lot but for you I would wish it otherwise. It grieves me to think that in your old age you must live away from your children with none to care for your comfort but strangers, and if I live long enough it shall not always be so. I do not get along *fast*, cannot earn much but I hope to do something for you. Do not work when you do not feel able to do so. I cannot bear to think that you must work as long as you can crawl and I do wish that it could be different.

If I thought I could make a decent living at C[laremont] I would come back there but I have tried to my satisfaction and must work where I can get more pay. I am very tired and must not stop to write any more. My love to all friends.

Most affectionately,
Your daughter,
Mary

North American Phalanx, N.J.

Sunday morn May 7th 1854
Dear father

I feel that you must be anxious to hear from me, and so will write a few lines that you may know that I am here safe and well.

I left, or we left Lowell the day I wrote you from there.[37] We had a very pleasant passage to New York, arrived there about eight-o'clock Thursday morning. Carrie & I were too tired to go about the city much so we did not see many of the "Lions". We left N.Y. for this place at three o'clock Thursday afternoon, instead of staying over night in N.Y. as we intended when we left Lowell and it was well that we did for

---

36. By this date Henry Paul was living in Lowell and was employed in the Lowell Machine Shop. Lowell *Directory*, 1853, 1855.

37. The letter referred to here has not been preserved. The reference makes it clear, however, that Mary had not left her Lowell experience entirely behind her.

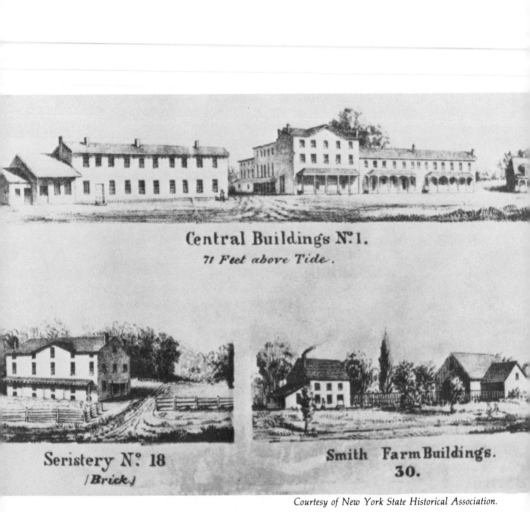

Central Buildings Nº 1.
71 Feet above Tide.

Seristery Nº 18
[Brick]

Smith Farm Buildings.
30.

North American Phalanx, 1855.

there has not been a *day since* when it would have been *pleasant* or even
comfortable on the water. You have of course read the acc't of the severe
gale of that day which sunk the "Ericsson" in the harbor of New York.
We very fortunately escaped the hardest of it. The boat had just
reached the landing, when the wind began to blow tremendously and
the rain to pour in torrents. The lifeboats blew off the top of the boat
into the dock and frightened many of the horses which were attached
to coaches which were standing on the wharf waiting for passengers.
There was no serious damage done as I have heard, though many of
the carriages came very near being overturned into the dock. We staid
in the boat until the rain abated somewhat and *then* took the coach for
this place. The rain came on again shortly and we got the hardest of
the shower on our way. The ride seemed a long one & the prospect
before us anything but encouraging (behind ditto) for our trunks were
on the rack of the coach without the least covering or protection from
the rain. Thus we rode ten miles or more over a rough hard road. I
thought *Redbank* sure enough for the earth when *wet* is as *red* as any
brick I ever saw.[38] It is mostly sand. It forms a very pretty contrast with
the bright green grass above. By the way it is spring here, peach trees
are out of blossom, cherry & appletrees are in full glory. As far as I
can see from the window, at which I am writing, nothing but immense
orchards of peach, cherry & appletrees present themselves to view. I
never saw *orchards* before, but I have got a long way from my story. I'll
go back. Well we arrived here a good deal *wet* & were kindly received,
had been expected for a long time they told us. The first thing attended
to was getting off our wet things and getting some supper. This over
we looked to our trunks; nothing in them was much injured though a
great many things were wet. So far we were comfortable, and finally
we have been that ever since we came, though we have had many
discouragements. Our things which should have been here with us did
not come until Monday afterward and then not all of them. We have
been very busy all the week putting things to rights. Have not done
much work beside our own. I have worked about two hours each day
for the Phalanx, three quarters in sweeping, one and a quarter in the
dining hall, clearing & laying the tables. Tomorrow I am going to begin
sewing which will add three hours each day to my work. On ironing
days I shall iron one, two or three hours just as I like. I must prepare
to go to my dinner now. We have one hour, from 12 to 1, for dinner,
breakfast from 5 1/2 to 7, tea from 6 1/2 to 7 1/2. After dinner from

38. Redbank, N.J., was the location of the North American Phalanx.

one till quarter past two I do my work in the dining hall. Three o'clock, I have come back to finish my letter. I cannot tell you anything definite now about matters and things because I dont know about them myself. I shall write you again as soon as I can & then I will tell you more about ways here. The place is very pleasant and the people remarkably kind. Upon the whole I think that I may like very well after I get used to the strange ways. That which seems oddest is the manner in which the meals are conducted. I believe I told you about it when I was at C[laremont]. I want you to write me as soon as you can, tell Julius to write. My love to him and Uncle Jerrys family and all who enquire for me. I shall write to Henry today and to William as soon as I can. Take care of yourself and dont work too hard. I wish that you could be here. I think you might find enough at your work to keep you busy as many hours in a day as you would want to work. There are a few here who work at one kind of business all the time but it is from choice. My work in the sewing room is to make a certain part of a stock (gentleman's stock). They make a great many of them here. Dont fail to write soon. I shall be anxious until I hear from you.

Yours truly,

Bela Paul   Mary S Paul

Phalanx October 2nd 1854

Dear father

 Your letter of Sept. 10th reached me in due season, & I was really glad to hear that you were so well. Hope you will continue so.

 I received a letter from Henry last week saying he had heard from William &c which I was glad to hear. I shall write him again soon.

 I am getting along very well here, better than I should at sewing. I have averaged about 6 hours work per day through the month of Sept. I do not yet know how much I shall have for it but I find I can live here easier & work but *half* the time than away from here & work *all* the time. Besides I am convinced that the work I do is better for my health than sewing. I have not done any sewing of any consequence & shall not be likely to have a great deal to do beside my own & there is always enough of that. I presume we shall stay here through the winter if no longer but we cannot decide that question until the end of the present month. Then Frank will know what the prospect is for him. Carrie is now in New York, *has* been two weeks with Emma who is sick of bilious fever. She was on her way from the White Mountains, got as far as New York and was unable to get any farther. She is getting better but probably will not be able to go home for a week or two longer & Carrie will stay with her, I suppose until she is able to go home.

When I wrote you before I think peaches were the *go* but they are all gone & forgotten now I expect. The sweet potatoes are being gathered now. They raise a great many here & we have plenty of them to eat. Three weeks ago yesterday the "mill" was burned to the ground. This was a *great* loss to the Association and puts them back in all their work as well as their plans. I do not know what the actual loss was but believe it was about $6,000. There were $3,000 worth of grain burned. There were several kinds of business carried on beside the milling, in the building, & the tools connected with them belonged to *individuals*. Some of the losses are heavy. They have about decided to build again, on the old spot.

I suppose William & Olive have returned from their journey to Lynn, bid they enjoy it.[39] I hope to hear from you again soon. How are Uncle Jerry's family & how does Julius get along? I wish he would write to me. I must not stop to write any more tonight for I must go to bed. I wait on the tables in the morning now & have to be up in good season. Love to all.

Write soon.

Affectionately yours,
Mary S Paul

———————

Phalanx New Jersey March 3rd [18]55

My dear father

I have been wishing to write you for some time but was prevented by the state of affairs here, at least I did not wish to write until I had something definite to say respecting my prospects here. But the probability is that I shall not *know* at present how affairs are to terminate, so I will wait no longer. I expect what I have just written needs a bit of an explanation. I think I wrote you early in the winter that the loss of the mill involved the Association in difficulties from which it would be hard to extricate it. That fear seemed to pass away and many seemed to think the foundations were too firm to be shaken even by an enormous debt, but it seems these were wrong for this

39. The reference here is probably to William and Olive Kimball, with whom Bela and Mary Paul lived in 1850. As a shoemaker Kimball may have gone to Lynn to return finished shoes and pick up additional leather stock.

Association is most certainly in the very last stage. I am sorry to say it but there appears to be no hope and a year at the farthest will terminate the existence of the North American Phalanx, in all probability. I do not know how long I can stay here but I shall not leave until I am obliged to do. The life here has many attractions & advantages which no other life can have, and imperfect as it is I have already seen enough to convince me that Association is the true life. And although all the attempts that have ever yet been made towards it have been failures, inasmuch as they have passed away (but they have all left their mark) my faith in the principles is as strong as ever, stronger if possible. There is a better day coming for the world. "We may not live to see the day But Earth shall glisten in the ray of the good time coming." Dont be worried about me, father, for I am certainly more comfortable here than I could be anywhere else. I suppose when I leave here I shall have to take up sewing again as that seems to be the only thing open to me. I flattered myself that I had fairly escaped from the confinement of the needle, but I shall have to return to it after all. Well I expect it will be all for the best. I was glad dear father to learn from your letter that you were so comfortable and I hope soon to hear that you are still more so. Oh that it were in my power to provide a comfortable home for you. A few days since I rec'd a letter from Wm. He was well and apparently doing well. Said he had intended to have sent you some money long ago but had been unfortunate about getting it etc., but would send you some yet. His wife is in Nashville at her fathers. He wished to be remembered to you when I wrote you. I presume you will hear from him soon if he has not already written. Frank & Carrie are still at South Orange & will remain for the present. Frank seems to be improving under the treatment. The weather is very fine here now. It seems more like May than March. I have in a glass of water, buds of the Mayflower which I got in the woods the 21st of Feb. Does'nt that seem like Spring? I want to hear from you very much & I hope you will write as soon as you can. I cannot think of Julius without the heartache. I wish I could do something for him. I wish he would answer my letter. Give my love to everybody that cares for me and accept the same for yourself from

Your affectionate daughter
Mary S Paul

Phalanx, April 12th, 1855

Dear Father

I intended to have written you before this time but I thought likely you had heard of me by Henry so would not be worrying about me. I suppose he has told you that I can remain where I am for the present through the summer probably, at any rate until my probation has expired. It is not at all likely that the Association will exist in its present form more than a year longer at most. A good many of the members have already gone away and others are preparing to leave.

From your last letter I perceive you have a very erroneous idea of affairs here. You say the place of interest seems to be in the hands of capitalists who have lost their courage when the hard times came. In this you are wrong. To be sure a good many of the stockholders are rich men, but the man who hold $2000 of stock has no more control than the one who only has $100, but of course he is the greater loser if his stock does not pay. It is true that many have lost their courage in the hard times but it is no more the rich man than the poor one. There have been many false steps taken & in a life like this which is but an experiment of itself there must be many failures, since man is not perfect. I know many will exult in the downfall of this place, but each are shortsighted. Charles Fouriers doctrines, although they may contain many absurd ideas, have enough of truth in them to keep them alive until the world shall be ready for them, and I am confident that it will take more than one lecture from "Dr. Lothrop" to annihilate Fourierism. Why I can mention any number of Associationists in Boston even who are just as strong in the faith as ever, confident as the "Herald" seems to be.

Oh there is one thing I intended to have spoken of when I was on the subject. I said, the man who had $100 of stock had as much control as one who had $2000. Perhaps you will ask if one who has *no* stock has as much. Yes in everything excepting in choice of public officers, and I suppose you can see the justice of that, but then, I know of but *one* member here who is not a stockholder, and I hardly think the privilege is denied him, for although he is poor he is very useful & probably that balances his deficiency in *money*. I guess I have said enough on this subject for the present.

Carrie & Frank spent a few days here last week. Frank is better but not well enough to take hold of hard work, therefore they are going to return to Lowell, soon. They have nothing in prospective to do but are in hopes to find something light which [will] not injure Frank & still afford them a living. It look rather dark for them, still I hope

something good will come of it. I am sorry to hear of Cousin Lois'
misfortune. The poor girl is having a hard time. I hope she get better
of this attack. Oh there is a remedy for rheumatism that a lady here
told me of. I was telling her about your case & she told me to tell you
to take *steam* baths, in this way. When you feel the lameness coming
on, have a *sheet* wrung out of *hot* water and wrap it about you. Then
over that put flannel blankets and dont spare the clothes. The object is
to produce heavy perspiration and thus throw off the disease. Half an
hour is long enough to remain in the sheet. On coming out of it take a
warm bath and rub till the flesh is dry. I have never heard of this
remedy before but I have a great deal of faith in it and I do wish you
would try it. You will find but little trouble I think, anyway I will pay
anyone who will assist you, give it a fair trial. How is Julius? I am
hoping to hear something encouraging of him. Give my love to him if
you see him, also to all who inquire. We have had a *very* backward
Spring here thus far, a great deal of cold weather. Planting has been
going on briskly for a good many weeks, still everything will be late.
The grass is now quite green but it should have been so weeks ago.
    Write soon, and believe me ever

Your affectionate daughter

Mary

Bela Paul

═══════════════

Phalanx June 11th 1855

Dear Father
    I dont know but you will think I am "strayed away or stolen" it is so
long since I have written you but I assure you I am safe & sound.
Before Henry came I waited to hear from him & since I have been so
busy that I have hardly thought of pen or paper. I was very glad to see
him. He came two weeks ago today (Monday) & left Wednesday
morning. I presume he has got fairly initiated into his work before this
time. I am expecting a letter from him every mail. I was very glad
indeed to get Julius' letter by Henry. It was a very good one. Tell him I
will answer it before long. When you wrote me last I concluded you
had not received my last letter, but from Henry I learned that you did
get it finally. I do not see why my letters should be missent as I
suppose they are for I direct them as plainly as I can. The weather is &
has been cool all the spring. We have had but a few really warm days
as yet. Neither has vegetation suffered from dry weather as it has East
according to reports. Everything is in good condition, potatoes are in

blossom & everything else as forward. Strawberries ripened late but we are having them soon in great abundance.

Yesterday 2,000 baskets (measuring half a pint each) were sent to market. They were all picked in one day on the domain. I presume as many or more will be sent today. All kinds of fruit are going to be as plenty as strawberries they say. Tell Olive I wish she could come out here & make us some strawberry shortcakes. I know they would be appreciated here. I am going to try to coax the cook to make one for me. I have all the strawberries I want to eat & it is the first time in my life that I was ever so favored. I went out one day & picked 20 baskets, but made myself almost sick by doing it. It is much harder picking them where they are cultivated than wild ones because they grow so closely it is hard to avoid stepping on them & then they are all picked clear of the hulls, and are ready for market as they are picked. This saves handling & crushing.

I suppose you recollect George Brewster of Woodstock.[40] He used to work for Eaton with you I believe, at any rate he used to know you. He is here with his wife. She was Frances Richmond, a niece of Walker Richmond. I think she told me her mother married a Shepherd for her second husband. I presume I have seen Mrs. Brewster & W[alker] but do not recollect her. She recollects you & knows everybody in Woodstock I should judge by what she says. They are travelling for pleasure I expect and came here to *see* as people go to Niagara to see. They are real nice folks but seem rather countryfied in their ideas. They have been married seven years, but Mrs. Brewster is still distributing her *wedding* cards.

Henry tells me you had not heard from William. I think it strange he does not write to you. I shall write him soon. How are Uncle Jerrys family? My love to them all, also to Uncle Seths family. Tell Cousin Seth I have not seen the letter he was to have sent me. I have tried to write coarse & plainly so it would not trouble you to read but I dont know as I have succeeded. I dont know how long I can stay here but for the present I suppose but what I shall do & where I shall go when I go away is more than I can guess. Write as soon as you can & as often as you feel like it. Dont wait for me. I will write when I can. I always want to hear from you & dont care how often.

Yours affectionately
Mary S Paul

---

40. This would be Woodstock, Vt., where Mary stayed briefly with her aunt and uncle before entering the Lowell mills, and where the Pauls had lived earlier.

East Unity [N.H.] Oct. 8th 1856[41]

Dear Father

I guess you will begin to think I write you often enough but I am living at the *Post Office* now and can send as many letters as I please if I only *pay* for them. The folks that Maroa & I are keeping house for keep the P.O. in their kitchen.[42] They went away this morning & are coming back Friday. I got your note with the enclosed letter Monday morning. I am sorry to hear that you have not found a room yet. What are you going to do? You must not stay in that damp place. Cant you find another place to *sleep* and let your *things* be there, that would be better than nothing. Give my love to Julius if he is with you now. I hope he will go back to Acworth again if he can get a living there & I suppose he does get that.[43] This mornings mail brought me a letter from Henry. He says he expects to go to Memphis, but does not know certainly, has not heard from Wm. since he wrote you, so there is no news from him. I presume we may *not* expect to hear from him (Wm.) until he gets his family moved to M[emphis].

The reason for my sending this letter now is to tell you if a bundle should come for me from Isaac—and I expect there will be one before many days—to send it by stage to Unity Village as I shall be there in a day or two.[44] I expect Mr. Glidden after me Friday or Sat. You had better direct the bundles to his care. I dont know what the bundle will be, but it would not be out of the way to tell the driver to keep it *dry* if possible.

My eyes trouble me some but I dont think they will be any worse. Write often, and get out of that damp hole if possible.

Love to all,

Affectionately,
Mary S Paul

———————

Manchester [N.H.] June 28th 1857

Dear Father

I suppose you will think soon that it is about time for another letter from me so I['ll] write, although I have little or nothing to say. The

41. East Unity is just south of Claremont, so Mary was living quite close to her father at this date.
42. This is probably the same Maroa whom Henry Paul marries. See below the letters of April 11, 1861, and after.
43. Acworth, N.H. is the next town south of Unity and is only about ten miles from Claremont.
44. This is the first reference to Isaac Guild whom Mary Paul marries in October 1857.

weather seems to be the principal topic here—its unusual coolness—but of course its all the same at Claremont so I wont waste time on that.

I wrote Maroa last Sunday and if you have seen her within a few days I presume she told you what news she had of me. My eyes are just about as they have been, or perhaps I ought to say better for they were *worse* than usual for several weeks. They are now about as they were when I came here.

I had my teeth fixed a short time ago and feel as if it were a good job done, though I hated to spare the money. I wanted it so much for something else, but my teeth needed it very much so I paid it out for them. It is quite warm today, seems like Summer. I want to hear from the boys, think it *very* strange that Henry dont write.

You said in your last letter that you had got your new vest & pants. Dont stop there, get a *hat* & *coat*, you need them.

I am glad you are thinking of going to Woodstock. Dont put it off, go right away, and go to Barnard with the little Tablet—if you can.[45] Isaac often speaks about it and once said he would have it put up, but I told him no. Give my love to Friends at Woodstock if you go before I write again.

Tell Maroa to direct when she writes me to C.F. Livingston's care. I forgot it when I wrote her. Give my love to her & to Julius, also to all who care for me.

Write soon and often

Yours affectionately
Mary S Paul

Lynn Dec. 27, 1857[46]

Dear Father

Perhaps you begin to think it is a thing to be doubted whether you have a daughter in these parts or not. I'll settle the matter however for the present by giving written proof of my existence. I am so busy all the time that I do not write any letters at all. I got very tired doing my work and sometimes think I shall not be able to do it. I think though that I shall find it easier when I get more accustomed to it. I was very sorry to hear that you were lame again. Hope you are better by this time. I wish you could be here with me, comfortably stowed away in

45. The tablet here is probably a marble slab intended to mark the grave of Mary's mother, Mary Briggs Paul, who died in Barnard in 1841.
46. This is Mary's first letter from Lynn, Mass. after her marriage to Isaac Guild on October 7, 1857. He was a marbleworker in both Lowell and Lynn.

my little bedroom where I could look after you a little when you needed it. Where is Henry now? He wrote me from Unity a fortnight ago. I suppose I shall not see him again before his return to Ohio. I wish he could come this way and make me another visit but I suppose that is hardly to be expected.

The ground is now for the first time this year covered with snow, but it will soon melt away I suppose in a few hours of bright sunshine. We have had very little cold weather but there is time yet to make it all up. I have not written Wm. for a long time, am thinking of doing so today if I can. I have a severe cold which makes one feel rather uncomfortably. Remember me to all friends who ask for me. Love to Julius. Tell him to write to me. Write soon.

Yours affectionately,
Mary P Guild

Isaac sends regards. M.

[Lynn] Monday Eve., Nov. 29, 1858

Dear Father

It is some time since I wrote you, still I have not much of interest to write about. The world jogs on and we jog with it, taking our share of what life has to give. We are well and comfortable for which we cannot be too thankful. I wish every one could say as much.

We had a little snowstorm yesterday, traces of which still remain. Sleighs have been running all day though wheels run more easily than runners as yet, I think. We see nothing of Henry as yet. I should [think] Maroa would grow tired of putting of[f] so many times from month to month. I am sorry Henry finds so much trouble in getting his money. It is very unfortunate for him. I hear nothing of William either. He may be waiting to hear from me though I wrote him last. Isaac's business is dull now as it is always at this time of year, but he will keep busy, getting out work for Spring. It is already past ten oclock and I ought to be in bed, so I must not write any more. I hope to hear from you soon. I am glad you had the thick vest made and hope you will have some warm *undershirts* & drawers. Dont neglect to get them. Keep as warm as you can.

Love to Julius & all friends.

Affectionately Yours
Mary P Guild

Lynn March 6th 1859

Dear Father

I learn by Aunt Betsey that you are willing to come to Lynn for awhile and I hope to welcome you to my home before many weeks. I think the necessary arrangements cannot be made short of three weeks or thereabouts. I do not wish you feel troubled or anxious about coming here. I wish you to feel free & contented & as much at home as if you owned the premises and I hope you will never allow yourself to feel for a moment that you are a burden to anyone. Henry and William will defray all your expenses and be *glad* to.

There is one thing which I owe it to Isaac to speak of & which I hope you will not take unkindly. As you are coming into a new place where nothing is known of your previous life can you not for your own sake as well as for Isaacs and mine refrain from that one habit which always brings naught but trouble & an ill name? I do not wish to reproach you with the habit nor blame you in any way. I only ask you to regard your own reputation & ours. I would not ask you to do this if it were *only* a matter of reputation & did not involve a principle of right. It is right for you to do it. Do not be offended with me dear father. I have only done what duty demanded of me.[47]

I shall come to Claremont & come down with you. I think this would be the best way. Keep up good spirits and dont worry yourself to death. Lynn is not a bad place, and my home is a much pleasanter place than your damp room. I shall not need any of your bedding & you had better not bring anything but your clothing and such things as you will want with you.

I must close now. Give my love to Julius.

Yours affectionately

Mary P Guild

Lynn April 11th 1861

Dear Father,

Let us make you acquainted with your grandson Irving Tracy Guild.[48]

47. While Mary is deliberately vague here, she is probably concerned about her father's drinking. The Temperance Movement was strong in Massachusetts, with many communities passing local prohibition ordinances in the 1850s.

48. Irving Tracy Guild was born December 30, 1860. Massachusetts Bureau of Vital Records, vol. 132, p. 268. The note at the bottom of this letter, "sent with Irving's picture," was added in pencil at a later date. The picture was probably a daguerrotype or tintype.

We thought you and Henry & Maroa would like to see the boy, so we send him along.

We are all well.

Yours aff'ly
Isaac Orr and M P Guild

[sent with Irving's picture]

Lynn Oct. 27, 1861

Dear Father

I presume that by this time you have got back to Windsor again so I shall send this there.[49] I was glad to get your letter and hope you will favor us often in the same way.

Soon after your letter came, one arrived from Henry, announcing the advent of a daughter to his house & home. I rejoice in his good fortune and I dare say you all do. We consider our boy the best gift that has ever been bestowed on us, and we try to take the best of care of that gift.

He is a healthy happy boy thus far, full of life and strength. I know it would do your heart good to see him and I wish you could. He is not as *large* now in *proportion* as he was 3 months ago but he is strong. He is not handsome but *good* looking, and we are very well satisfied with him and hope he will grow up to be a *good* man.

You will find the [Lynn] "Reporter" which we send this week badly crumpled with his little fingers. He is not allowed to have papers but he laid violent hands on this one, so we send it to Grandpa for a message.

I have been wondering whether Julius went with the Fifth N.H. Reg't.[50] Let me know when you find out. I suppose he thought it his duty to go, but I am sorry. I hope *nothing* will ever induce Henry to go. Isaac of course will never go as he is a nonresistant in principle.[51] Henry is fortunate in haveing work in these hard times but I hope he wont kill himself at overwork. Isaac has absolutely nothing to do and

49. This is the first letter addressed to Bela Paul in Windsor, Vt., located just across the Connecticut River from Claremont. Henry Paul and his wife Maroa were apparently also living there, as is clear in the next letter in the series, in which Mary offers advice to them in bringing up their daughter.
50. In fact, both Julius and Henry Paul served in the Army during the Civil War. See Otis Waite, *History of the Town of Claremont, New Hampshire* (Manchester, N.H.: John B. Clarke, 1895), pp. 277, 280.
51. Isaac Guild may have been a Quaker, hence his position as a non-resistant. Lynn had an outspoken Quaker group throughout the antebellum years.

winter coming & a family to support. He is not very well but better than he has been, and I am not well either. Shall have to keep a girl all winter I am afraid. That is, if we can manage to pay her. We have a house now at 72 dollars a year, which is better than paying one hundred though our rooms are smaller & fewer in number. I shall do my own work as soon as ever I am able to and I hope that will be before a great while.

I am afraid you wont be able to read this it is so poorly written but it tires me very much to write and that will account partly for the writing if it is worse than usual. I hope this will find you all as well as can be & I hope also that some of you will write me soon and let me know how Maroa and the baby are getting along. Love to all.

Yours affectionately
M P Guild

Lynn April 27th 1862

Dear Father

I meant to write you weeks ago, but I have been so nearly tired out that I have put it off hoping to feel stronger, but it is of no use. I never felt so nearly used up as now. I have had no "girl" since January and Isaac and I have managed after a fashion to get along. He has had so little to do that he could help me a great deal about my work. I could not have got along at all only for him.

We made another move April 1st and I hope we are settled to stay for some time where we are. We were very much crowded for room where we were and what was worse the house was so situated as to get almost no sunshine at all in Winter, and that circumstance alone would prevent our staying in it any longer than necessity compelled. We have plenty of air & sunshine where we are now, and larger & better rooms though the same *number* of them. We live *up stairs* as usual. I wish we could afford to live in a lower tenement, it is so hard for me to do my work up stairs though I manage not to go over the stairs more than once or twice a day because I have to be saving of my strength.[52] Irving is nicely as usual and a great comfort to me as well as a great trouble, for he has to be watched so closely to keep him out of mischief. He dont talk any but is going to one of these days I suppose though we are in no hurry to have him. I had made up my mind to make you a

52. Mary Paul was five months pregnant at this date. On August 31, 1862, she gave birth to a second son, Sidney Pratt Guild. Massachusetts Bureau of Vital Records, vol. 150, p. 230.

visit this Spring, but the times are so hard, and the trouble of taking a child on such a journey so much, that I have decided to wait a little longer but I shall come as soon as I can with any comfort to myself and you. I want to see you all very much. I hope little Mary is thriving, dont play with her too much, and dont *feed* her too much (to H[enry] & M[aroa]) if you wish her to get along comfortably through "teething." My boy lives *entirely* on oatmeal gruel (cooked six or seven hours) with a little cream for breakfast & supper and *rye mush* (well cooked) with a little cream & sugar for dinner, half a graham cracker for luncheon in the middle of the forenoon. This will probably be his diet until he gets all his teeth, which will be a long time for he has only *six* now. There may be, and doubtless are ways of managing babies, as good as mine but I am sure that the more simple and *unvaried* their food for the first three years of their life the better. I dont know anything of Julius, and I suppose there is no reason to expect anything from Wm. at present. I hope though he will come out all right when the end comes. I hope you are all well and will write as soon as you can. Cousin Seth called to see us last month. I forgot to tell you where we are living now, on Essex St., cor. of Washington, west side of Essex & north side of Washington. You'll find it easily enough. Write soon, love to all.

Yours affectionately,

M P Guild

Delia Page, c. 1860.

FOUR

Delia Page Letters

THE LETTERS of the Trussell family to Delia Page while she worked at the Amoskeag Manufacturing Company in Manchester, New Hampshire, offer a unique perspective on the mill experience of young women in the antebellum period. They provide a glimpse of that experience from the viewpoint of family members who remained at home. Only three of Delia Page's letters to her foster family have survived, but a careful reading of letters she received permits a partial reconstruction of her life in Manchester. More importantly, the letters give us a sense of how family members reacted to Delia's experience as she shared it with them in her half of the correspondence.

This collection is far larger than any of the others reprinted here, consisting of more than 120 letters, most dating from a nineteen-month period between October 1859 and May 1861. Almost all of the letters were written by Delia's foster parents or sisters while she worked in Manchester. They tried to write weekly in time for the Friday stagecoach. On many occasions several family members wrote to Delia at once and there is considerable repetition in the letters. I have included here about a third of the letters, minimizing repetition and yet still giving a feel for the range of letters Delia received in this period.[1]

Born in 1841, the eighth child of John and Miriam Page, Delia had been living off and on with Luther and Eliza Trussell for a number of years before she found employment in the Manchester mills. Her mother died shortly after her birth and her father remarried two years later. Delia apparently had a poor relationship with her stepmother, something she alludes to at several points in her correspondence.[2]

1. Trussell Family Papers, Town Archives, Tracy Memorial Library, New London, N.H. Letters and diaries used and letters reprinted by permission of Mildred Crockett Tunis.
2. For family information on Delia Page see: Myra B. Lord, *A History of the Town of New London, Merrimack County, New Hampshire, 1799-1899* (Concord,

When Delia moved in with the Trussells is unclear, but it appears to have been well before her entrance into the mills of the Amoskeag Company. Several pieces of evidence are instructive here. First, the enumerator for the 1850 census of New London recorded her residing in two households, with her father and stepmother and with the Trussells. Sometime later that year John Page and his family moved to nearby Newport, although his son Anthony and married daughter Harriet continued to reside in New London. Delia corresponded with the Trussells, and an 1855 letter suggests she may have returned to live with them that winter. She wrote in a postscript: "Father said I might come down to your house and go to the winter school. If I come I shall be down the middle of November. I am so glad ain't you Mother? I shant come back again I tell you."[3]

Whether she ever returned to her family in Newport is uncertain, but she did attend school in New London for three years. According to her own accounting, Delia attended the district school in New London for three winter terms and the private academy there for two spring and two fall terms. Annual catalogs of the New London Literary and Scientific Institution note her attendance between 1856 and 1858. After this period of schooling, Delia worked out for about a year before she entered the Amoskeag mills in the fall of 1859.[4]

Economics do not appear to have played much of a role in Delia's decision to enter the mills. Both the Trussell and Page families were prosperous. In 1860 Luther Trussell paid local taxes on property valued at more than $3300, including 125 acres of land, bank stock, and $1200 in money on hand. The Pages were even wealthier. John Page owned real estate in 1850 valued at $2500 and had another $2100 at interest. His widow in 1860 had real and personal property worth more than $7000.[5] Delia's brothers owned substantial amounts of property in their own right, and when the family sold a farm in New London in December

N.H.: Rumford Press, 1899), pp. 368-69; Edmund Wheeler, *The History of Newport, New Hampshire, from 1766 to 1878 With a Genealogical Register* (Concord, N.H.: Republican Press Association, 1879), pp. 487-88.

3. For the enumerations of the Page and Trussell families see 1850 Census of New London, dwellings 142 and 93; 1860 census: New London, dwelling 191; Newport, dwellings 449 and 450. Delia's letter to Luther and Eliza Trussell, dated Sept. 16, 1855, is not reprinted below.

4. Delia Page to Luther Trussell, Jan. 22, 1860, see below; *Third Annual Catalog of the Officers and Students of the New London Literary and Scientific Institution,* (1856), p. 14; see also 1857 *Catalog,* p. 14, 1858 *Catalog,* p. 16. On Delia's employment, see below Delia Page to Luther M. Trussell, Jan. 22, 1860.

5. Invoice of Local Taxes, New London, 1850 and 1860; 1860 Census of Newport, dwelling 450.

1860, Delia's share came to $571. She had ample funds for a marriage portion.

A desire for personal social and economic independence rather than economic need sent Delia Page into the Manchester mills. Her 1855 letter indicated that she did not want to return to her family, and her father's death in February 1859 must have sealed that decision. At the same time she would not have wanted to be dependent on the charity of her foster parents. She had some inheritance coming to her, as Luther Trussell's letters make clear, but there were numerous complications and she could not know when the estate would be settled. Even when she learned of her share of the sale of the family's New London farm she did not give up her mill work.

We do not know how long Delia worked at the Amoskeag Company in Manchester. Judging from the letters from her foster family and a diary kept by Sarah Trussell, Delia worked off and on in Manchester from October 1859 until at least sometime in 1862.[6] She may in fact have worked until 1866 when she married Charles Thompson. The new couple did not remain long in New Hampshire, however, as Delia wrote a letter to her foster family from Tomales, California, in July 1867. She returned to New London on visits at least twice, in the summer of 1872 and fall 1874, according to a journal kept by her foster sister, Mary Trussell. There are occasional references to her husband but no indication as to any children.[7]

The most interesting aspect of this correspondence, and what makes it unique among letters of mill workers that I have found, is the evidence it provides about Delia's social life in Manchester, and the anxiety it caused her family. The letters, beginning with one written by Luther Trussell on August 24, 1860, reveal that Delia was having an "affair" with a fellow mill worker, Sylvester Drew. She wrote her foster sister that she was "desperately in love." On inquiring of Manchester friends, whose letters survive in this collection, the Trussells learned that Drew was married and had deserted his wife and child in Lowell. They forwarded this information to Delia and implored her to think seriously of the likely consequences of her attachment. To escape the supervision of her boarding-house keeper, Delia apparently took up new lodgings, probably in a

6. Sarah Trussell Diary, June 20 and Oct. 3, 1861, Tracy Memorial Library, New London, N.H.

7. Three letters written by Delia from California to the Trussells have survived but have not been included among those reprinted below. On Delia's visits to the Trussells, see entries of July 15, 1872, Jan. 1, Nov. 11, 1873, Oct. 20, 1874, Mary Trussell Diary. Tracing in California censuses has failed to find Delia and her husband.

private home unconnected to the corporation. Their Manchester infor-
mant wrote the Trussells that Delia and Drew visited one another in the
mills, and were "creating a good deal of talk." A close reading of the
letters suggests that Delia returned home to her foster family for a while
in the fall of 1860, and after she resumed work in Manchester her foster
father expressed his relief that she had overcome her "dreaded trouble
with so little dificulty."[8]

After November 1860, Delia evidently continued to see Drew, though
her passion appears to have cooled. Her foster parents, for instance, no
longer focused their letters on this issue. Sarah Trussell, however, recorded in her diary that Delia and Ida Drew, Sylvester's 7-year-old
daughter, came home to New London in June 1861, and stayed fifteen
weeks before returning to Manchester. Drew, described by Sarah as
"Delia's man," visited New London in late August. Regrettably, however,
the diary is quite brief and tells us nothing substantive about Delia and
Drew.[9]

The Drew episode as revealed in these letters is symptomatic of
broader changes in courtship and marriage that occurred in the nineteenth century. In this respect, Delia's experience is probably not at all
unusual. Daniel Scott Smith, using evidence drawn from Hingham, Massachusetts, has argued that parents' power over the marriages of their
children declined in these years. Earlier, marriages had more the character of compacts between families; by the mid-nineteenth century, individual choice had greater rein. Mill women, like Delia Page, represent
one end of this spectrum, and the opportunities that mill employment
offered undoubtedly contributed to the overall decline in parental power
over marriage choices that Smith has described.[10]

The letters to Delia Page highlight some of the problems families must
have experienced when their daughters entered the mills in the antebellum years. Given the distance that separated young women from their
families, they had a measure of social and economic independence that
must have made parents anxious at times. They would have met men,
perhaps even chosen marriage partners, with little knowledge or influence on their parents' part. That Delia evidently shared her emotions
with the Trussells may well have been a result of the fact that they were

8. See letters below, especially Luther Trussell to Delia Page, Aug. 24, Sept.
7, 11, Nov. 16, 1860; Sarah Trussell to Delia Page, Aug. 29, 1860; B.H. Piper
and R.M. Piper to Luther Trussell, Sept. 4 and 20, 1860.
9. Sarah Trussell Diary, June 20, Aug. 22 and 23, 1861.
10. "Parental Power and Marriage Patterns: An Analysis of Historical Trends
in Hingham, Massachusetts," *Journal of Marriage and the Family* (1973), 35:419-
28.

her *foster* family. They exerted their influence in letters which in the end appear to have been successful—Delia did after all marry Charles Thompson, a respectable, single man. In any event, work in the textile mills separated young women from their families and permitted them to grow and change in ways that may well have disturbed those back home in the countryside. We are fortunate to gain access into one dimension of this cultural conflict in the letters of the Trussell family to Delia Page.

New London Oct. 9 [1859]

Dear Delia,

I was very glad to hear from you, and hope you will continue to get along well.

We went to Concord last Tuesday.[11] I enjoyed the ride down very much. We reached Mr. Eastmans at 2 PM. I was hardly seated before they inquired about you (I guess they take quite a fancy to you).

At 3 we went to the Street. I got a pair of Auricles, price $5 and a pair of green spectacles which I like very much and several other articles.[12]

We came home the next day and such a winding I never got before, but strange to say we didnt [feel] the least cold.

Are you as well suited as ever with the Port[r]ait?[13]

Write again soon

Yours Truely,

Sarah E Trussell

New London Oct. 19/59

My dear Girl

You think strange that we have not answered your letter sooner but from some cause or other it did not reach us untill last night.

Now you would like some news there is a great scarcity of the article

11. Concord is thirty miles southeast of New London, and the Trussells probably went by wagon to nearby Potter Place and then by train to Concord. The Northern Railroad offered train service to Concord as early as 1849.

12. Sarah Trussell, Delia's fifteen-year-old foster sister, had eye problems and probably purchased the dark glasses to protect them from the sun. The auricle would have been an ear trumpet to improve her hearing.

13. Sarah did quite a lot of painting, as becomes evident in later letters. Here she is probably referring to a portrait of Delia she painted before Delia had gone to Amoskeag.

The Trussell Farm, c. 1860, as painted by Sarah Trussell.

at this time as the high wind on Thursday blew every thing of this nature far out of town excep such gross stuf as is too heavy to be transmitted by mail. I will send all I can pick up.

Mr. Craft & wife have been to Hopkinton had a glorious time.[14] Sarah & I have been to Concord she has a pair of Glasses & a set of Auricles and thinks she can see & hear finally well. George Knowlton has gone to Sutton to meeting & Eliza has gone here.[15]

Uncle Amoses last girl (I dont know her name) was married thursday they had a big wedding.[16] 60 couple more or less I think were invited. How many attended I have not heard.

I am pleased to hear that you & Miss Pattee stil board at Mr Clements and that you have called on Mr. & Mrs. Piper.[17] When you next see them give our respects to them for I think them not onely entitled to our respect but our Gratitude. I am glad too that you have changed your work as I think it will not be so Fatiguing and I am more afraid of your doing too much than not enought.

Take the work easy until you get accustomed to it then put on the speed. Sarah has written you but Mary is too unwell to write today. She sends her love & says she will write next time. With my best wishes I am yours to serv

Luther M. Trussell

P S Your mother was going to write to you but has not time. She has been working & in the midst of it we had company (Thomas Nichols of Boston and his wife). Aunt Savage (who is also his aunt) is coming up tonight with Hiram so excuse us & write again soon.

Yours L[uther M Trussell]

---

14. The Crafts lived in an ell of the Trussell homestead. George Craft owned a stage line that served New London. The family moved from the Trussell place in the spring of 1860 but continued to live in New London and was enumerated in dwelling 29 in the 1860 Census.

15. George Knowlton is a cousin and boarder in the Trussell household at this time. Sutton is the town just south of New London. The others mentioned here are Eliza Trussell, Luther's wife and, later in this letter, his younger daughter, thirteen-year-old Mary.

16. Amos Page is an uncle of Delia. His youngest daughter, Mary, married Daniel Annis of Londonderry and continued to reside in New London. Lord, *History of New London*, pp. 272–73.

17. Mr. and Mrs. Piper are Benjamin and Rosaline Piper, acquaintances of the Trussells in Manchester. Rosaline Gile Piper was a New London native; Lord, *History of New London*, p. 251. Later, when the Trussells are concerned about Delia they write the Pipers for information. Miss Pattee may have been a daughter of Isaac and Martha Pattee of New London. In 1860 two sisters, Arvilla and Mary, fourteen and seven years old respectively, resided at home with their parents, in dwelling 16.

New London Novmr 11 1859

My Dear Girl,

We received a couple of [news]papers last Thursday & suppose they came from you. I hope you will find time to write soon as the papers were quite silent as to your whereabouts, business or health. I was glad to see them and thank you heartily.

Our school closed Wednesday. Kate went home Tuesday morning, Dickinson Wednesday & Richardson & George Thursday so you see we are quite alone again.[18]

They had a fine exhibition Tuesday night and Wednesday night there was an Antique party at the Flat.[19] The object was to obtain the needful to purchase a seraphim. They acted Miles Standish courtship and John Aldens *Marriage*. Eliza, Sarah, Mary, and Capt. Andrews folks went with his large waggon.[20]

Sarah painted 17 pictures on glass to put into the fare, Mary knit a scarf for her part sold $1 1/2. They realized about one hundred dollars besid a good time (they borrowed S[arah's] large pictures to hang up in the hall). Mr. Bouton of Concord was their biggest man.

I suppose you have plenty of amusement as well as employment and if you are well you ought to be happy.

We are in comfortable health and employd as usual. Mrs. Joseph Messer, daughter of Stephen Whittier, was buried thursday she died of fever; 33 yrs old & respected by all who knew her.

If you have not already heard it I will inform you that Anthony has bought Mr. Hows farm.[21] Mr. How is going to live with his mother.

Edwin intends to purchase what there is of your fathers place not appropriated by his widow. They value it at $1600. Your part will of course be about $145.[22]

18. These four were probably boarders with the Trussells during the school term at the New London Literary and Scientific Institution. Founded as the New London Academy in 1838, this private school had been known by a number of names. I will follow the Trussells' usage and refer to it in notes as the Academy.

19. The Flat is Wilmot Flat, the town adjoining New London to the southeast.

20. Capt. Andrews is Benjamin N. Andrews, a near neighbor of the Trussells. Two of his children, Martha and Mary, are mentioned periodically in the letters. See dwelling 189, 1860 Census.

21. Anthony is an older brother of Delia, living in New London at this date. According to Luther Trussell's letter of Dec. 15, 1859, Anthony moved to Newport, fifteen miles west of New London, where the remainder of the Page family resided. As becomes clear in the letters, Delia's father has died recently, and much of Luther Trussell's correspondence with Delia concerns the settlement of his estate.

22. Edwin, twenty-two at this date, is another of Delia's brothers. Delia's mother died just after her birth and her father remarried. Thus his widow is Delia's stepmother.

The farm west side of the town is not sold for want of a purchaser, but if you have your health you are doubtless as happy as any of the family & may soon be as independent from the avails of your own labour.[23] Write soon

Luther M. Trussell

New London Dec. 4, 1859
Dear Delia

It is the Sabbath and we are detained from meting by a smart snowstorm. We would [like] to know whether you are at meting; or what you are engached in to day. We trust you attend meting always when you can. We often think of you, with sincere desires for your welfare. Your paper reaches us weekly. We look upon it as a token of your kind regard for us; and while we would express our gratitude, we think it most too hevy a tax for you.

We would like to know all about you. What is the state of your health? How is that lame arm? Many are the questions we would ask. I think you can anticipate most of them; so when you write, please answer as many as you can.

You, doubtless, wish to know how we are. Sarah was better last week than she had been for a long time, but to day she is worse. I think she has taken cold. Her father too is ill. I hope both will be better tomorrow.

Dec. 6. I cannot spend much time in writing to day, so I will just say remember the advise we have heretofore given you, as it is the same we would now give. How well we would like to look in and see you but as this cannot be write and tell us all. Accept our love and best wishes.

Your foster mother,
Eliza S. Trussell.

New London Decmr 5th 1859
Dear Delia

We received your papers in good time & thank you for them. They are pretty good for the kind. But in point of true value I think them

23. Luther Trussell is probably referring to a larger farm in New London owned by the Pages. The family sold that farm a year later and Delia's share of the proceeds amounted to $571. Luther Trussell to Delia Page, Dec. 6, 1860.

inferior to Life Illustrated.[24] I am afraid you did not have time to read them yourself. I advise you to take some paper or periodical that you can have leisure to read and if you can keep the good & cast the bad away you may be continually improving your education. No one should ever dream their education is finished when they stop going to school. Education ought to be long as life. We can if we try be growing wiser & better every day. After you have read the papers send them to us if you like. We shal not value them the less for having contributed to your improvement.

I have seen quite a number of your connection within a few days.[25] They were & are all well as far as I know.

We have had quite a little winter. It was good sleighing most of last week. Saturday the snow left us but Saturday night & Sunday gave us a foot of new. It is 5 PM the trees are covered with ice and it has been very foggy all day. It is too dark to write. Be a good girl. Try to excell in everything you do. Take care of your health, save your earnings. And remember always that you are a Steward and must give an account of your Stewardship. With my warmest wishes for your happiness and prosperity, present and future. Goodbye.

Luther M. Trussell.

[Dec. 5, 1859]

Dear Delia,

I take this opportunity to write to you. I attend school this winter; Mr. Colby keeps; I like him very much, he aint much cross, scolds some to the little children, and I wish he wo[u]ld to some of the larger ones, they need it bad enough. Some of them complane of him for being slow (some will complane ennyway) but I like him much; to be sure he never hurries and thare no need of it. I suppose you are at work in the mill as happy as can be. How is your arm which was so numb when you left home?

Do you kno wether Helenna Colby workes in the mill at M[anchester]? Miss Holbrook said she did a while a go. Your Kitty Gray ran away about three weeks ago; we none of us know whare he went (perhaps he went after you). Susan Craft keeps school on Kings

24. *Life Illustrated*, founded in 1854, was an inexpensive weekly, described as a miscellany of "entertainment, improvement and progress." Frank Luther Mott, *A History of American Magazines, 1850-1865* (Cambridge, Mass.: Harvard University Press, 1977), p. 42.
25. "Connection" is used here in the sense of relative.

Hill.[26] She gets a long nicely. But as I think of nothing more to tell you now, I will close. Good night. Write soon to me.

from your affeccinate,

Sister Mary

Delia M. Page

Manchester, N.H.

P.S. I thought I would write and tell you some more about Kitty Gray; he went away before the snow came. We suppose he found a good home which he liked and so did not return, we did not kill him.

Mary

===

New London Dec. 10, 1859

Dear Delia

We have this afternoon received your kind letter, good paper, and very pretty present. Accept our sincere thanks for all. You certainly do not forget the folks at home, this is truly gratifying.

From the tone of your letter, I judge you are enjoying yourself quite well and doing well too. I do not think so much of your making great wages, as of your keeping good company, and being a good girl. Be sure to attend meting constantly on the Sabbath, unless prevented by sickness. Our love to your good Methodist friends. I suppose you generally attend that meting. Write about it in your next. Jr. Hunting has been waiting to see me ever since I have been writing so no more at present.

Dec. 13. I am afraid you will get sick. You must have a very hard time. Do try and take care of your health.

Sarah Call is at home sick of a fever.[27] I believe thus think her a little better. She has been very sick.

We would like very much if you could come in and spend a few hours with us now and then, but as this can not be, write often, and if you cannot, send a paper.

Heaven bless you my child.

Yours affectionately

Eliza S. Trussell.

===

26. Susan Craft was a daughter of George Craft and is recorded as a schoolteacher in the 1860 census, dwelling 29. The Trussell home faced west across a valley toward King's Hill in the western part of New London.

27. Sarah may have been the daughter of Reuben and Sarah Call, recorded in dwelling 87 in the 1860 Census of New London. Sarah, a schoolmate of Mary Trussell, did not recover and died shortly thereafter. Mary Trussell to Delia Page, Jan. 5, 1860.

New London Decmr 15/59

My dear Delia,

It is past 9:00 PM but I will write a few lines in hopes to send them in the Morning. We thank you for yr paper tis very good but I am afraid you had not time to read it yourself & the knife was a beauty and will ever remind us of the donor.

I think of you every morning when I come down & see the clock often an hour after you have been at work.[28] You must retire early and try to get sufficient sleep and rest. Take care of your health whatever els goes uncared for and if you find you are getting too tired go to Mr Pipers or come home & rest you.

I have not much news. Anthony is moving to Newport & has sent over here your part of the wheat raised past season Viz one bushel, one quart & one pint & a fraction. That is what I understood [from] Mr. Craft. I have not measured it yet. Now I am going to tell you to be a good Girl for I think you are but continue to be good and as much better as you can.

There is a hard snowstorm out doors and I think it doubtful whether this goes for several days.

Luther M. Trussell

Delia M Page

[Dec. 28, 1859]

My dear Delia,

The girls have written and your mother would but that she has the headache. We have just reread your last paper & I again thank you for it. But the Dollar Monthly you mention (though I doubt not that it is a interesting periodical) I think we do not need as we now have eight different papers which certainly ought to be enough. I am glad to see by this offer that you are in a condition to do somewhat as you are amind to and it must be a very pleasant feeling. It is a thing much to be desired to be able to rely upon yourself with Gods blessing for all the necessaries of life. If you have not already attained to this independence I think you soon will & that too without any great help from your father.[29]

28. Delia probably worked the standard hours in the mills. If so, she averaged sixty-six hours, working six days a week. Monday through Friday work lasted from 6:00 A.M. until 6:00 P.M. with a half hour break for dinner. Saturday was a shorter day, bringing the weekly total to sixty-six hours.
29. Trussell is suggesting here that Delia will be able to support herself independent of the inheritance she can expect from her father's estate.

It was very cold here this morning twenty degrees below zero (zero now). When you can conveniently let us know what you are doing and how much you clear a week. We feel much interest in the matter as we know you work hard for all you get.[30]

I must leave off and read your paper which I have not yet looked at. So good night til next week.

Luther M. Trussell

New London Dec 30

Dear Delia,

I shold hav finished on the other sheat but since Father has written it nearly over. It is a very cold day and it storms hard [,] so hard I could not get to school. I have been two days this week. I hope I shal go more next. I get a long nicely at school.

I went to the Laydies Public meeting last night. They had a very good one and a very good dialogue. It was of old times. The subject of it was Thares many a slip twixt the cup and the lip. They had an old fashiond quilting party. They were fitting out a girl to be married. It was Mary C. Clements. She acted her part very well. They all did. When the time came for her to be married she was all dressed. The brides maids wer there, everything was redy when they found out the gentleman she was to marry had married another; and so it came out that there is many a slip between the cup and the lip. Miss Rogers done the most about composing it of enny one. Miss Holebrook was an old grandmother. She had had a dream and others had seen and heard things wich made them think that she mite not get married.

I suppose we may expect something very nice in our next paper. We do think so much of them and we are all so very *very* thankful to you for them.

I wish I could see you a while if but a little while but I guess you will think I have written a nuf. Please excuse all mistakes. I send a large share of love to you.

Goodbye.

From your Sister Mary

We intended to send your letter today but it stormed so that we could not get to the Post ofic.

---

30. Unfortunately the Amoskeag Company payroll records for this period have not survived, so we cannot determine exactly how much Delia was earning.

New London Jan 14, 1860

Dear Delia,

We were sorry to learn that you had been ill, but it was what we feared from your delay in writing. You will probably take cold more easily now than before. Do take all the care you can to prevent it, lest you get the feaver. We have thought much about you lately. When we herd of the Lawrence catastrophe, we immediately thought of you.[31] How dreadful! How many hearts are wrung with anguish to day! What would have been *our* feelings had you been among the sufferers! And what would have been your present condition? How important that we should live prepared to meet death at any moment! "For in such an hour as ye think not the Son of man commeth."

Do seek, without delay, an interest in the Saviour. It will not diminish your happiness in this life, and without it you cannot be prepared for the life to come. Nothing, nothing is half so important as an interest in Christ. It is indeed "the one thing needful." Nothing will compare with that in importance. May you so seek as (soon) to find; is the prayer of

> Your foster mother
> Eliza S. Trussell.

P.S. Mr. Dunbar and a boy are here, and the talking has disturbed me since I have been writing.

> E.S.T.

N.B. Write once a week when convenient, but be sure to write once a fortnight unless prevented by illness.

New London Jany. 20th 1860

My dear little factory girl,

I have written a long letter to you but I have laid it up so safe I cant find it so I will write this long or short as it may be. We are very glad to hear that you are doing so well, but dont do too much. Take care of your health at all events. You will oblige me if you will take time to answer a few questions which I shal ask by & by. Your friends or some of them think that your father done a great deel for you & now I wish them to know just what he did do & what he did not. So I want you to state:

31. On January 10, 1860, the Pemberton mill in Lawrence, Mass., collapsed. The accident and resulting fire killed eighty-eight people and seriously injured more than a hundred. Donald Cole, *Immigrant City: Lawrence, Massachusetts, 1846-1921* (Chapel Hill: University of North Carolina Press, 1963), pp. 31-32.

1. What cloothes you brought here from NP [Newport] when you came here to go to school: dresses, ptcoats & drawrs & shirts and whether they were new or not.[32]

2. How many termes you attended the Academy.

3. How many weeks you have worked out at the various places & times since you came here before you went to Manchester.

4. What ever your father has given you since you came from NP up to the time of his death.

Recapitulated

1. What cloothes 2 how long at the Academy

3. How long you worked out

4. Whatever your father has given you since you came here.

Take a little time and answer it as correctly as you can. It cant do you or anybody any hurt & may do you & I some good and you may send the answer on a seperate half sheet with your name under it.

We will try to keep you posted in the affairs about home by writing once a week. You must write us often as you can get time & feel like it.

Luther M. Trussell

Manchester N.H. Jan 22/60

Dear father,

I received your letters last evening, and will now try and answer your questions as well as I can. When I came from Newport, as you very well know, I had but a very few clothes. I had but three dresses, one delaine and two calico for underclothes. I had but three pairs of drawrs, three chemise, one quilt, and two white skirts. I had two cheap shawls, and a sack which Emily gave me.[33] Mrs. Page (she isn't my mother and I wont call her so) bought me a shawl in the summer and paid between one and two dollars for it, and the other I swapped one that I had when I went there or rather I let Alice have it and I knit some feeting and father paid a little and got it.[34] I did not have any winter bonnet only one that they got me in summer and paid $2.25 for it. I had two pairs of shoes. I believe that is all, but mind you, I knit

---

32. Luther poses these questions to Delia in anticipation of a court case he has pending. As becomes clear in later letters he has a claim against the estate of Delia's father for support he provided Delia while she attended school in New London. As Delia's brothers are opposing his claim he writes her for evidence to buttress his argument that he, rather than her father, has provided most of her support since she left her family.

33. Emily is a sister, seven years older than Delia.

34. Alice is a younger sister who would have been eleven at this date.

ten dollars worth of feeting. I dont know as they call that anything but I do, dont you? Now about the school. I went to the Academy part of two spring terms, 8 weeks each, and two fall terms. I went to the district school three winters and one summer. I worked to Mr. Carrs 24 weeks, the next year I went to Hopkinton. Next I went to Croydon and worked two weeks. From there to Lebanon and stayed 15 weeks then I came home.[35] I had a lame wrist. I went to Newport that winter and staid to fathers a few weeks. I presume they will charge for my board. You remember father gave me $15.00 at one time. There is something else. He gave me a dress and his wife gave me a few rolls and $3.00 besides. But why need they make such a fuss? Isnt it a fathers duty to take care of his children until they are able to take care of themselves? But I have not had my share of the rent and the rest have but I shall be provided for.[36] I will not borrow any trouble. I have written all that will be necessary. I will write to Mary. So your little factory girl will bid you good bye. Write soon.

Delia M. Page

Luther M. Trussell
New London, N.H.

New London Febr 22d/60

My Dear Girl,

If you had no letters last week you will have enough this to make it all up. I wrote you on Sunday and again Tuesday morning. And now I write again lest you should not get the last written.

I thank you for the confidence you manifest in me and assure you it shal not be abused.

But to come to the matter in question. Mr. McCucheon told the Heirs last summer that I had a claim on the estate (based on the agreement with your father). And they as he said directed him not to pay one cent.[37]

35. Here Delia is noting the various places she has worked, probably between the end of her schooling and entrance into the Amoskeag mills. Croydon is ten miles and Lebanon twenty miles northwest of New London; Hopkinton is twenty-two miles southeast.

36. The Page family owned a farm in New London that they rented out until its sale in December 1860. As one of her father's heirs, Delia feels entitled to a share of the rent, hence her comments here.

37. Luther McCutchins was a leading resident in New London, a successful storekeeper and farmer. He may have been appointed executor of John Page's estate, hence the reference to his dealings with Luther Trussell and the Page heirs. Lord, *History of New London*, pp. 359-61.

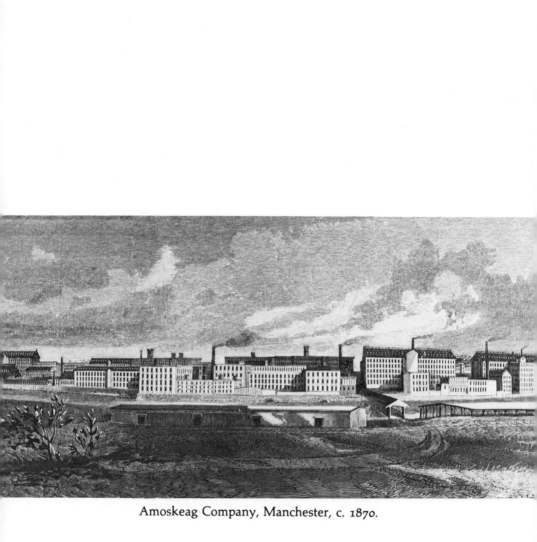

Amoskeag Company, Manchester, c. 1870.

After this Monroe & Anthony saw me and Anthony told me I had no business to have done anything for you.[38] That I was meddling with what did not concern me when I went to Croydon when you were sick. That they would not pay one cent if it cost him all his share. The Croydon affair which irritated him so much was not & is not in the account nor any mention made of it.

As he defied me to get anything I told him I should take whatever the commissioner should decree. So here it rests. I would have settled any time by the agreement made with your father. But settle they would not.

Most if not all your Brothers & Sisters have had more than you some of them I believe as much as 3 or 4 hund[red] dollars. You have been cheated because there was no one to look things up for you. And they seem disposed to continue the same course by getting you to come up on their business at your expense & loss to time which all together could not be less than ten dollars. And this to help them cheat me.

Mr. Jewet has exposed himself to an action for damages if first hand [illegible]. The commissioner will set three days I suppose, the first, the 25th the other days conciderable later but I have not been informed when though I think the last day is the fore part of June.

I do not know whether I shal go over Saturday or not, at all events there will not be much done the first day. If this affair troubles you it disturbs your mother as much. She had rather give up everything & has tried to prevent me from doing anything. But I believe it is my duty to get a just settlement if I can & that is all I want.

As to your coming up. It cannot be of any use. And you had better not have anything to do with it unless you are legally summoned. You will surely get into trouble if you come. The Lawyers will make you say things you will be sorry for, & I shal have to have you up on my account if you go for them. They have not heretofore manifested much interest in your wellfare and I believe they would be willing to fleece you to any amount without much compunction of concience.

Give yourself no trouble about the business. I will protect your rights and the others have no doubt of their ability to guard theirs.

I have the satisfaction to think my dear that you have a clearer perception of justice than seems to actuate your connections and this I attribute whether correctly or not to the influence of your Mother

38. Monroe is probably James Munroe Jewett, husband of Delia's oldest sister, Harriet Page. He lived in New London at this date. Lord, *History of New London*, p. 369; New London Invoices of Local Taxes, 1850-1860.

Trussell. It is my earnest prayer that you may ever possess it for it will always be for your interest as well as happiness to do right.

And now with a hearty God bless & preserve my Dear Girl I will bid you Good bye.

L.M. Trussell

NB Remember not to come up to court or commence settlement. Let who will come after you unless you are legally summoned (and any one bringing you up otherways will be prosecuted according to law). Indeed keep clear if you can by any means.

Luther M Trussell

New London March 9th/60

My Dear Girl,

I did not expect to write you untill next week but circumstances are such that I shal anticipate the time a little. Your mother has worried ever since you went away fearing you took cold and are sick. I don't believe you are sick but with her I am sorry you did not have a better breakfast. I have not much to write as there has not much transpired since you left.[39]

Elex. Jones 2nd child died on Wednesday of croup and the Babe left by Mrs. Bunker the same day. George Everett was thought to be dead yesterday for some time but revived (probabely had a fit). A poor English boy named William Wood came here on Wednesday in the snow storm ragged, sick & discouraged. Your mother mended his cloathes & doctored him up so that now he is quite smart & happy. I have written to Mr Peters to have him help him.[40] He is a good boy & worth helping. He will tell you what he can do or thinks best for William to do & you can let me know in your next which I hope to receive Monday or Tuesday. Dont forget to write all about my little factory girl & tell her to remember all her father said to her when she was at home. We are in usual health.

As I do not know Mr Peters Christian name I have simply put on Peters. Please hand it to him.

Luther M Trussell

D M Page

---

39. Delia has apparently been back to New London since the letter of February 22, perhaps to attend the first court hearing.
40. Mr. Peters appears to be an acquaintance of Luther Trussell who resides in Manchester. The Trussells wrote first to him and then to Benjamin Piper who eventually helped William Wood get a job in Manchester. There are

New London March 16th/60

My Dear little factory Girl,

We were very glad to hear from you but sorry Mr Peters did not get his share of your letter.

All I wanted Mr Peters to do was to find a place for the lad in the mill. He will recommend himself if he has oportunity. As he has neither money nor friends he does not stand a very good chance to get in at once and he has no funds to wait upon.

Enclosed is a Letter to Mr Piper I would have written to him direct had I known his christien name. Please hand it to him soon as convinient.

The news is mostly of a political nature. Gov Colby goes Rep[resentative] by 62 majority.[41] Mr. Craft is going to move out soon and Mr French will take his place.[42] Mr Prescot goes to Hanover. Mr Fowler comes in his place. Mr Crocket is moving to the Hobbs place.[43] I have seen Monroe & Edwin to day. they are well but say Mom Page is rather unwell. Your other friends at NP are in usual health.

Sarah sends her love to you and is in hopes her eyes are getting better though very slowly. Mary is writing you but I think she will not get the letter finished in season for the mail.

Your mother & I Bless you. So good bye my dear Girl

Luther M Trussell

New London March 23d/60

My ever Dear Girl,

We are always glad to hear from you. But your last letter was thrice wellcome for the information it contained. As I do not know the

periodic references in the letters to Wood who eventually repaid the money the Trussells advanced him and returned to England.

41. Governor Colby was Anthony Colby, a member of one of New London's founding families and an incorporator of the Academy. He represented New London in the state legislature between 1828 and 1839, was elected Governor in 1846, and returned to the General Court in 1860. Lord, *History of New London*, p. 230.

42. The French family lived in the ell of the Trussell homestead and according to the census included John and Catherine and a son, William.

43. Charles Crockett purchased the Hobbs farm, immediately adjoining the Trussells, and operated it as a diary farm. In 1889 his son Oren bought the Trussell place and combined the two farms. Lord, *History of New London*, pp. 457, 580-81. His daughter, Mildred Crockett Tunis, continues to reside there and has kindly permitted the transcribing and editing of the letters reprinted here.

address of Mr. Peters I am under the necesity of sending William to you and you can give him directions how to find Mr Peters.

As he cannot read writing you must be sure he understands and see that he finds the proper places and persons. We have helped him to Manchester and I must trouble you to see that he is made acquainted with Mr Peters and when convenient with Mr Piper also. He is a good boy and will make friends when he has oportunity. (I wish *you* could learn him to *read* & *write*.)

You spoke of the commission court at N[ew]Port. Give yourself no trouble about it. I will assertain what they must do to oblige you to attend and write you word in good season.

The old farm of your mothers is sold to Edm[und] Davis for 1350 dollars. I have got to go to NP before I can make out a deed for your share.

We are as well as usual. We always want to hear from you often. And now we shal want to know how William Wood prospers too. And we can onely hear from him through your pen.

When you have leisure write us a long letter. Begin when you have a mind to & write as you have oportunity. Be sure to have it long. You need not doubt but that it will be interesting to us.

The rest cant write now.

Luther M Trussell

My good Factory Girl
P.S. I forgot to say that Mr. Crafts folks have moved to Georges & Mr. French has come in his place. Remember me to Mr. & Mrs. Piper. Tel him I thank him for what he has done for William & wish him to take him to meeting & to his meeting too. His father is a Methodist & I wish him to be.

Dear Sister,

I have just returned from school; I have been rooming with Kate this week I havent been a *mite* homesick.[44] I enjoy my self very well. I cant believe nearly six weeks of school have passed.

The laydies had a public meeting last night. I think (and all I have herd say enny thing about it say the same) it was the best they ever

---

44. This would have been Kate Story, a cousin, who also attended the Academy. Kate and Mary probably roomed together in the Ladies' Boarding House.

had. O it was so good and the Fisherville Band came over and played
for them and Mr. Crutching James escorted them.[45]

But I cant write much so Good by. Write soon to your affectionate
sister

Mary

New London May 9/60

Dear Sister Delia,

With much impacents I awaited the arrival of the stage Sataday
afternoon. At last it *"hove in sight.'* My heart beat quicker. It turned up
the steps and Enos[46] handed me a large pacage which at first glance I
knew was a book. I went into the house and opened it carefully as you
directed and out droped a bosom pin. *It is a little beauty.* It sutes me
exactly. Then I looked at the book and behold it was Cowpers poetical
works jest what I wanted in fact I am delighted with my presents.[47] I
thank you a thousand times for it, and I hope that some time I shall be
able to paint you a picture which you you will like as well as I do my
book and pin.

Yours very truly

S.E. Trussell

Prof. Gardner has got a little girl about a week old.[48]

New London May 9th /60

My dear girl,

You requested me to take some rainy day & write you a long letter. I
am tired of waiting for the rain and think you would be for the letter.

We have just received your last letter[,] likeness and money. We all
thank you for the picture.[49] I think it is a pretty good one. But I am

45. Fisherville was an industrial suburb of Concord about twenty-five miles
from New London.
46. Enos Craft was the stagedriver in his father's business.
47. William Cowper (1731-1800), an English poet, collaborated with John
Newton, a Calvinist preacher, on *Olney Hymns* and produced several volumes
of letters and poetry.
48. George Gardner, a "teacher of language," lived with his wife and three
children and was enumerated in the 1860 census of New London, dwelling
28. He was principal of the Academy between 1853 and 1861. Henry Rowe, *A
Centennial History, 1837-1937: Colby Academy, Colby Junior College* (New London,
N.H.: Colby Junior College, 1937), p. 88.
49. Although it is impossible to be certain, this picture may be the ambrotype
which has survived and is reprinted at the beginning of this collection.

afraid William has not yet got cloathes sufficient & to pay me (he must care for himself first).[50] Sarah got your kind & valuable presents. Nothing could have pleased her better they are just the thing.

You would not have had a pleasant visit at Hopk[into]n if you had gone up. George Eliza & Mary went down and found on their arrival Mrs. Savage dieing. She lived but three hours after they got there. They stayed to the funerall and came home on Monday.

Joseph C. Messer, brother to Richard, is buried this afternoon. 35 masons attended in uniform they have just gone back (died of consumption).[51] You want a long letter but I have no news to write. I know nothing about the people at NP [Newport]. Shal not probably go there till the last of June. I have applied for licence to sell all your real estat both here and at NP and shall see as soon as there is a good oportunity.

It is extremely dry & vegetation is not so forward by ten days as at Manchester. The Canida plumb wild cherry & sugar plumb have not yet opened their blosoms. We have set out quite a number of shade trees this spring & with much care I hope to make them live.

Friday May 11th. I have nothing new worth reading. I am at work on appletrees, planting and painting and almost everything else.

L M Trussell

D M Page

[May 9, 1860]

Dear Delia,

I thank you for your good letter. How good it seems to get a letter from you every week. It seems to lessen very much the distance between us. I have just been looking at your ambrotype. I think you have not changed in looks for the worse since you left us and I trust you have not in any other respect.

Give my love to William. I was really sorry to see the two dollars he sent us. I think he must need the monney himself. One thing I should like he should send us sometime an ambrotype of himself.

May heven bless both you and him. Continue to be a good girl and

50. Judging from this and later letters it appears that William Wood is returning the money advanced to him when he went to Manchester. Soon after he returned to England.

51. The freemasons were members of a secret fraternal organization of British origin that was established in the American colonies in the 1730s. King Solomon's Lodge, No. 14, was founded in New London in 1802. Lord, *History of New London*, pp. 706-14.

seek above all things an interest in Christ for the best must have this or perish at last.

Your mother Trussell

New London May 17th/60

My Ever Dear Girl,

    Your letter was a very welcome one & it contained a great curiosity. You have oportunities to see many things that you could not find in the country. It is in fact a good place to earn money and a very good place to spend it. Try & not spend too much. See how soon you can put twenty dollars in the bank and send me word of the event. I saw your uncle Amos yesterday. He enquired for you, said he was in Manchester this spring and that his folks said you were doing *well*. I am glad to hear a good report of you, not doubting that it is well deserved. This you have obtained by effort and continual unremitted effort can alone perpetuate it for you. It is my wish that you should be the best of your family, and effort enough on your part will surely make you such. So try, try again for in due time you will succeed if you faint not.

    Uncle Ezekiel was here yesterday. Maryette is quite sick again. He thinks she wont be any better. Marcia was thrown out of a waggon about four weeks ago and is not able to put her hands to her head.[52] The horse ran away with her broak the waggon to splinters and one of his legs so they had to kill him. I intended to write you a long letter but I have not time now besides Mary and your Mother have been writing so I think I will stop & carry this to the [post] office.

    P.S. I suppose you will want to know what I am doing. Well I am digging worms out of the apple trees. They, the trees are going to blosom well & I hope we shal have some apples for you this fall.

Yours
L M Trussell

My Dear Factory Girl

---

52. Ezekiel Trussell is an older brother of Luther who lived in nearby Wilmot at this date. Maryette is an unmarried daughter, twenty-nine at this date, while Marcia is a thirty-three-year-old married daughter also living in the area. Lord, *History of New London*, p. 394.

New London June 13th /60

My Dear Delia,

Your letter & papers arrived Mond[ay] evening. They were all very wellcome. So it seems you have got a deposit in the bank. You have done *well*; made a good beginning—a *very good Girl*. Now you can add to it as you are able and it will soon be sufficient to afford quite a pretty sum anually as interest. But my Dear Girl I believe you are working too hard. You must be careful or instead of 4 dol[lars] pr week you will not have anything.[53] Take care of your health whatever else goes uncared for.

Get all you realy need and earn all you can without injuring your health (practice economy in your expenses) do not get things merely because they are cheap or pretty). Save all you can of both Health & Money for *future use*.

We have little in the shape of news in fact I cannot think of any.

Mr. Marshall Hayes was here to day taking the census. I gave you in and all you had.[54] This is Thursday & there is a man here pedling that once worked in Manchester mills & lost his right arm by being caught in the machinery. He is from Newport. His name is Chase; says he knew your father. It has been very warm here today Thermom[eter] 86 in shade. We are about as well as usual though Sarah is pretty lame yet from the horse falling on her in the spring. Her eyes are some better but far from well. Mary goes to school and is hard drove at that. Your mother & I have all the comefort we can get at home. Eliza has the headach so she cant write. Now my good girl, practice all I have told you (that is good) and make any improvements that your wisdom may suggest. Good bye till next week.

L.M. Trussell

D M Page

Here is a little bit of fringe. It is deep enough but not thick or heavy enough. Your Mother wants it to put round the yoke of a black satin cape. She wants a yard and a half. We cant get any suitable here. If you can do so and send it up by Mrs. Piper.

I wish you to asertain the price of the galvanic batteries of Mr.

53. This wage of $4.00 per week was a bit above the mean for weavers at this date. In the same month, June 1860, women weavers at the Hamilton Company in Lowell earned $3.78 per week on average. Dublin, *Women at Work*, p. 162.

54. Delia Page was enumerated twice in the 1860 census, in the Trussell household and in her Manchester boardinghouse. See 1860 Census: New London, dwelling 191; Manchester, dwelling 86.

Tibbits and see if you know how to manage them.[55] I suppose I shal have to get one and if I was sure I could manage it I would have one at once.

Write & let us know all you wish and all we want to know if you can. Here is dollar for you to pay for the fringe with.

Good bye

L M Trussell

D M Page

Your mother says she must have black (not blue black) as nigh the shade of this peace of satin as you can get. And she further says you must not work yourself to death but come home before you are sick.

P.S. Your mother wants six triming buttons about the sise of a quarter of a dollar and the same shade as the fringe.

New London June 20

Dear Sister,

It being only Wednsday night we dont send our letters off till Fri. I thought I should have time to write a little to you. I am studying Latin and recite to Miss Forsaith after school. I genraly get my lessons at home nights and dont have much time to write.

You know I told you we had got a socity at our school. Well I am Pres. of it the next 3 weeks and Arvilla Pattie Sec.

I never enjoyed going to school so well a Summer before in my life as I know of. But I shall be glad when the fall term comences. I am going to it you know.

You sade you should be up in Sept. Then you think you can stand it through the Summer, we shal be glad to see you, very.

It seems then William wants to go back to Eng[land]. Well I thought when he was here he intended to stay in this country till he was 21 years of age. I shouldent think he would want to go home now if he ran away; not untill he has got some money. But I suppose his father would have it if he got it and if he drinks it would not do him any good.

There was a young man stayed here a few nightes ago that lost his right arm in the Manchester Mills. He was quite smart and could do a good deal of work with his left hand though you know it must be very inconvenyant to have but one arm and that his left.

---

55. The galvanic battery was an apparatus consisting of alternating silver and zinc strips wrapped in cloth dipped in a saturated salt solution used to generate electricity.

George was here last night and has gone over to his grandmothers to day. He is comeing back to morrow.

It has been very rainy to day and is blowing and raining now (9 1/4 oclock) with no signs of clearing away. I am sick of so much dull weather, aint you? But God knows what we need better than we do so I will try and not complain but be patient.

Isent it rather warm in the mill some days Delia? I should think it would be. I guess I shall go to the mill sometime in course of a year or two and get some money to buy a piano as I dont see much prospect of haveing one unless I do work for the money and I want one very much.

I suppose you have had strawberries before this time. They are just geting ripe now here.

I think my letter is geting rather long. Excuse me for writing with a lead pencil. I can write so much faster with one and easyer to.

Please write to me soon. We all send our love. Good night

Yours in love
Mary Knowlton T[russell]

> Forget me not
> Forget me never
> Till yonder sun has set forever
> Remember me when this you see
> And I'll remember you

Mary your sister

Delia M. Page
How many roommates have you now?

Your sister Mary

New London June 20th/60

My Dear absent girl,

Your letter & paper was punctual to time arriving Mond[ay] evening. We were very glad to receive them. It is a hard cold storm here today, a great deel of rain has fallen & the wind roars like an October gale. I think you will be much more comfortable in the City today than you would be here. I wish I could call in and see my little Factory girl. In deed I did rather think I might be there in Sept (but that would be uncertain) besides I hope you will be at home at that time. How came you to find out what was written on my last letter & erased? Sarah wrote it but I did not wish you to notice it. Dont pay any attention to it. You are doing quite enough now. Friday has come around again. I must finish this and put it in the office that you may not be disappointed in its reception. Thare is no news. Nobody dead or married.

P.S. Mother says you needent troubel yourself very much about those buttons. If you cant get eny that are right you needent get eny.

L[uther M Trussell]

New London June 28th/60

My Dear absent Girl,

We got the articles by Mrs. Piper (thank you).[56] Your letter and paper arrived on Monday night.

I was at Newport Monday. The business I went on was respecting what I had furnished You: Books, Cloathes, Tuition &c. You will want to know what was done. *Not much.* Probabely it will all amount to *nothing.* The widow Page, Edwin, Harriet and husband[,] Anthony & wife were there. Rosoline & Emily were not represented though I saw Mr. Herd in the street.[57] So there was a great deal *said.* I was called upon to state how & why you came from your fathers to live a second time with me. I stated the reasons. This affected the Widow very much. She immediately began to whine & sniffle and laid the blame all onto *You.* Anthonys wife supported her statements by telling how sausy you were when you lived with her & concluded by declaring that if one of her children talked to her as you youst to she would knock them down. The Widow declared that she *loved* you. They contrived however to give you anything but a good name. This I could not disprove but I told them that however bad you were when you came from them you were neither *lazy* nor *sausy* now, that you had the name of being a likely respectable girl and I knew it to be so.

They did not inquire your character in the opinion of any one. But if they did not damage their own it must be because people had a not very good one of them before. The gr[e]at object after proving you were *bad* was to make me *worse* by trying as they said to get you away & so was the cause of your acting so improperly at home. Had you been there you could have refuted this falshood but that would have made no difference in the end. And so far as I am concerned

---

56. It was a common practice in the antebellum period to send letters via a traveling friend to save postage. The Trussells sent letters and packages to Delia via Luther's cousin, Mrs. Haynes.

57. This would have been Delia's brother-in-law, Rial Hurd, husband of Emily Page. Lord, *History of New London,* p. 369.

personally I care but little how it goes. I intended if I got anything out of the estate above my expenses to let you have it towards making up what you have lost through your fathers means heretofore. It does seem as though they thought you was not a child and had no rights whatsoever as such.

I was asked by Monroe *why* it was your father gave you 15 dollars. I answered by asking him why yr. father gave his wife 100 dollars about the same (he did not choose to tell).

I am very glad to know you are so plesantly situated and enjoying yourself so well. Dont work to[o] hard & lay up all you can. You will not always be in a situation to earn so much. Take care of your health. And I hope you will long live to enjoy your own earnings and the society of your true friends.

L M Trussell

D M Page

New London July 5/60

Dear Sister Delia,

I received your letter Monday. I am glad you have not forgotten me. How did you spend the "Glorious Fourth"? Some of the schollars (Academy) tryed to take comfort and the consequence was that s[ome] of them were expeld and about a dozen more taken up. The way they took to get their comfort was as follows: They intended to go round in the night of the third and get all the horses they could and go off to a ride with out any ones knowing it. But some of them got so drunk that they "let the cat out of the bag," so they gave that idea up. About half past eleven in the night, they broke into the meeting house and began to ring the bells, when the folks heard them came and took them and locked them up in Colby Hall.[58] They sent for Mr. McCutchings and he went through some of the rooms at Colby and he sade some of them were fitted up equal to any barroom he ever saw with rum and sugar and lemonade and glasses and everything good to make them drunk. All those that they took up were worse for drink and all expeld were drunk. Mr. Knight found one dead drunk in the road. He got him to his room and locked him up. He waked about noon yesterday. Prof. Gardner sade that he wished them to understand that they were expeld for being beastly drunk. I dont know the names of all taken up, the only one you know is Charlie Page you know he is real pretty and

---

58. Colby Hall was the boys' dormitory at the Academy at this date.

quite smart. He would graduate this summer. He got drunk. His father died a drunkard but I hope Charlie wont be like him. They had a trial yesterday afternoon and put the boys under $200 bonds to appear at 9 oclock tomorrow. Squier Flanders from Wilmot Flat was lawyer. So much for the Fourth here. One thing more they have got our great flag up. Lincoln & Hamlin.[59] Oh aint it good. I did not go any where yesterday. Aunt Nancy was here. I could not but think where I was a year ago. O I remember just what I did and everything which happend so well. I went down to Grandmarm Trussells. She went out with me in the fields and I never had a better time in my life. I *never* shall forget what good times I have had at Grandmarms. We had mustard greens yesterday same as we did a year ago. I dont expect we has as good a time as you did but then we enjoyed ourselves well. Ed Stintson is up and is going to stay six weeks. He is some improved I guess. What is your picture which you had taken last? Was it Melenotype (I dont know how to spell it)?[60] I like it and Sarah and I and Mother I guess are going to have our pictures taken. Theres a man come in today to take them and I want mine taken like yours. Please when you write tell us what it is. What do you call that little mark you sent me? I dont know what to do with it unless I keep it to look at. I thank you for it, it was very pretty indeed. Jennie Cooch and Ernestine Huntoon were babtised Sunday. I went to the babtising with Mr. Crafts folks. John Hall carried us and a lot moer.

What a change there has been since you was hear but I like it pretty well. I miss Mr. Crafts folks very much and Mr. Prescotts too. But we have some very good people in there places. Mr. French has doen a great deal to the fenc and other things since he came here. Oh you cant think how much better it looks in the other part.[61] It is all paperd over and white washed and the west room is painted and paperd and carpeted and they have some real nice furniture in there. The house looks a great deel better. Old Grandmarm French is there. I like her so much but I wont praise them any more. You must come and see them for your self.

George has just come up from Sutton. I have not been to school to

59. Hannibal Hamlin was the Vice-Presidential candidate along with Lincoln on the Republican ticket in 1860. The Trussells were evidently Republican enthusiasts.

60. Melainotype was an early name for a tintype, a photograph made on a thin metal plate having a darkened surface. Robert Taft, *Photography and the American Scene* (New York: Dover, 1964), p. 156.

61. The "other part" mentioned here must have been the ell of the Trussells' house.

Colby Academy, c. 1865.

day for it rains and I am real *sick* of going to school. But I shal be glad when the Academy begins next fall.[62] I want to write a good deel more, but I have written a long letter so Goodby. Please write to me when you can for I like to have you very much. Sarah says that she will write to you when you write to her. She sends her love. Good by.

Yours in love
Mary your sister

New London July 15/60

Our Dear Sister Delia,

"I now take my pen in hand to let you know I am well, and hope you are the same." Oh did you ever in all your life see a letter commenced so. I know in "old times" they always did begin so, and a good many begin so now. I always hated it. Well, Father recieved your kind letter of Tuesday night; I am very sorry I must wate 3 long weeks for a letter. But patients!

School closed today and Oh, I am so glad. For I am sick of going, such trials and tribulations as we do have at school. Oh dear! I told you I belong to a socity at school well I am going to leave it. I left it to day. There are two partes in school. To the one I belong to belongs Arvilla Pattie, Emma Messer, Ella Allen and myself. All the boys are in favor of us and some large girls that dont go to school. We are pretty strong I think. To the other belongs the teacher, Angie Randlet, Carrie Seamans, Phebe Call, and Lillie Sargent. This partie feels so big I wont go with them.

I have had my minature taken again. I had a Melenotype taken & a Ambrotype one for Miss Rogers and one for our folks. I like the fun of having them taken. The artist is J. Foster. He looks a great deal like Mr. Tom Richardson (you know him) and I guess he is *some* like him.

They have not got through with the court yet about the 4th. The lawyers make their plea to night. They are all free and are now witnesses but the three they expeld.

Mother is going to send you a cheese. It is not a very good one but she has not made but 2 this year. She has the milk only every other day. I send a bouquet it was almost dark when I made it so you must arrange it over if you dont like it.

---

62. Mary appears to be attending the district school at this time and expresses her preference for the Academy. It was quite common for New London children to alternate terms in the public and private schools. Delia did the same herself; see her letter of Jan. 22, 1860, above.

I almost dread next week for I expect we shal have a good deal of company. I have a good mind to run off and stay with you next week.

We think Delia that why you dont tell when you think of coming home is so as to take us by suprise and see if we are glad to see you. Well we *shal* be *glad* to see you. You must come and see how you like the change around here. I like it well, though I liked them as they were.

But it is bed time in the country so I must bid you goodby. Good night. Remember me for you *see* I remember thee.

Write as soon as you can to

Your ever loveing true

Sister Mary

I am afraid fathers letter will be dry, it takes him so long to write it, he writes a line then thinks a *long* time then writes another so on "to the end of the chapter"! Dont forget that I write short letters. Folks wont know that your letters are always from the same person as they are not directed by the same. Dont be sick of reading my ribble rabble for my heart is full of love for my dear Delia. Good night. May you have pleasant dreams and be prospered in all things. Amen. Your true Mary.

Dont think I am crasy for I aint though I may wright as though I was.

Sat. morning July 14

The stage has gone and your things have not. I heard them comeing and ran in to get the box when I came out it was against the lower steps & they would neither see nor heare. I expected they would stop if Mrs. Piper was on board, whether she was or not I dont know. I am very sorry for although the things were of little value they had cost us considerable trouble and I know you must be greatly disappointed but I hope you will not feel a great deel worse than Eliza does. I could cry if it would do any good. I am going to try to get this through by the other stage.[63] So that you may have it tonight.

L M Trussell

D M Page

---

63. Two stage lines ran near New London, connecting to rail lines that joined in Concord, and went on to Manchester, thus giving the Trussells two ways to send letters and packages to Delia.

New London August 24th/60

My Dear Absent Girl,

We received your letter last night and were all glad to know that you are still in possession of health and happiness. Long very long may you possess these inestimable blessings. I have no doubt you enjoy life. Probably as well as you ever will, however happily you may be situated in the future.

Every state of our lives has its peculiar advantages. Every change of place and circumstance gives us something new something peculiarly its own. It may be agreable or disagreable pleasant or painful or what is most common a mixture of both but whatever it is in that situation it is unavoidable. You now feel & enjoy independence trusting to your own ability to procure whatever you want, leaning on no one no one depending on you. Change your condition by uniting your destiny to another (however good and great he may be) and this feeling is gone— *gone forever*. Whether that which follows will be more or less agreable depends entirely on the fitness of the union. And as this union is usually for life it is of the utmost consequence that we make a deliberate and wise choice.

That love is blind with one eye & sees but poorly with the other is undoubtedly true. We look upon the best side of those we love. And are apt to think that any little defect we cannot avoid seeing will easily be cured by our affection and wisdom.

But I assure you that a person, male or female, who persists in a habit known to be disagreable to another before marriage will be slow to mend their ways to please their companions afterwards.

I do not wish you (nor any one else) to be a morose old maid. But to be united to a companion who will enable them to be more *Respected*, more *Useful* and more happy than they otherways wo[u]ld be. Whether I come down or not, there are a few things I should try to understand before making up my opinion. First his charracter (We take it for granted his morrals are good). Is he a professor? Does he honor his profession? Is he industrious? Does he have few leisure days? Is he economical? Does he save his wages? Is he benevolent? Does he help those who cant help themselves? Is he kind to all? Patient with all? If all these questions can be truly answered in the affirmative, then he will be a blessing to any girl who deserves a good husband.

But you must not trust too much to your own judgment. Ask Mr. and Mrs. Piper. They can learn more about him in one hour than you could in six months. Take no steps without their knowledge and consent. For a mistake made in a moment may be lamented a lifetime.

Luther M Trussell

I do not think it likely that I shal come down (tis difficult getting a horse).[64]

———————

New London N.H. Aug. 29

Dear Sister Delia,

I received your kind letter Monday night, was verry glad to here from you.

You must excuse me if I dont write to you evry time for my eyes are so weak I cannot; they are not much if any better than they were two months ago.

So you are *"desperately* in love," I should like to know how you feel, pleas tell me in you next. Are you engaged? When are you agoing to be married? Is it very sickly in M[anchester]? Did that Jonson girl that died last Sabbath board at the same place you do? I have asked a good meny questions for I cant think much to write.

I have just received a request to be a Honorary Secretary of the Cosmopolitan Art Association for this year in this town and vicinity; or get some one to act in my stead, as they "are anxious to secure one in every community."

What do you think of that? I dont think that I can get but very few subscribers. People are so afraid of taking eny thing that is *worth* a taking, but I am agoing to try.

I cant think of eny thing else to write. There isent any news.

Yours truly

S.E. Trussell

———————

New London Aug[u]st 31/60

My Dear Girl,

Your letter to Sarah was duely received. And besides as you know I saw Miss Chadwick. She spoke in high terms of you, said you was a good girl very steady and earned more than she did or could. In the course of conversation I enquired if you had a Beau. She said not that she knew of. And though I told her nothing I could see her suspicions were excited.

I was highly gratefied with the good report I hear of you. But am afraid you have got rather too deep into *Love.* It is a dangerous place

64. From this postscript and the preceding letter it appears that Delia has informed her foster father about her relationship with Sylvester Drew and has asked for his approval. She seems to want him to come to Manchester to meet Drew, which request he feels unable or is unwilling to meet.

anyway, especially for Ladies. As in case of disaster they are generally the greatest if not the onely sufferer. Their female acquaintance[s] furnish but cool sympathy and non can be expected from the other sex.

Love is said to be an affair of the Heart but I have noticed that usually the Head is very much disturbed. Most of the senses are more or less affected and the Faculties especially the Judgment are entirely destroyed.

A fair appearing unprincipeld man can easily impose on an honest unsuspecting girl. And to one of your temperament there is more danger than to thos differently constituted. So that I must again caution you not to let your affection get the better of your discretion.

Of the Gentleman mentioned I know neither good or evil. But the circumstances which surround him are not such as to give me the most favourable opinion.

When ever you marry I wish there may be a reciprocal attachment found on merited esteem, ripened into *Love*. Such attachments are calm and enduring, and the longer and harder they were tried the stronger they would grow.

I know very well that Love laughs at reason and is deaf & blind to cause and effect. But do not act hastily. Reflect, consider. When once bound there are but two ways to be released. Neither plesant but either perhaps preferable to remaining as you then are.

Consult your friends. Do or say nothing you would be afraid or ashamed to have me know. And do not fail to give me all the information of your schemes, hopes & fears that the relation I stand in towards you warrents me to expect.

Luther M. Trussell

D M Page

Manchester Septr. 4/1860

Mr. Trussell
Dear Sir

I received a line from you in which you wished me to make certain inquireys about Sylvester Drew of Manchester.

I know not your motive in this inquireing on this subject, but it maters not. I will give you the information which I have gained and that is undoubted. Mr. Drew has a wife & one child in Lowell.[65] He has

---

65. Massachusetts Vital Records confirm the account here. Sylvester Drew married Elizabeth Best, Dec. 21, 1852, and a daughter, Ida F., was born Sept. 28, 1853. See MVR, 61:118 and 73:118.

ben trusteed twice by his wife, is also a man that drinks hard and also runing after other women, is a very unprincibled Man.[66] These facts I obtained from good and satisfactory authers.

Yours truley
B. H. Piper[67]

New London September 7th/60

My Dear Girl,

We received your welcome letter on Monday. The amount of inteligence is not very great or yet very clear. It seems you have changed your boarding place but I can only guess the reason.

You say too that you are not so desparately in Love. That I am *glad* to hear. I hope you will escape being in love at all with Mr. Drew. Perhaps you have learned more about him since you first wrote. Any way I will tell you some things you did not then mention but of the truth of which there can be no doubt.

He was never divorced but has a wife and child living in Lowel now. And his employers have been trusteed twice for their support. He is concidered very intemperate and has the reputation of being a Libertine and making *Love* to all ladies that favour him.

That you were deceived in regard to his charracter I have no doubt. For he is in fact far below Alfred Cutting (whose intentions were honorable though unwise). And nothing but *disgrace poverty misery* and *death* can be expected by any one so unfortunate as to be connected with him.

A person is known by the company he keeps. Therefore avoid him and all like him as you would the *Plague*.

There are no decrees about our happiness or our marriages. But all our future is put into the Talents given us and our happiness or unhappiness depends on the use we make of them.

Marriage was instituted by our Creator for our happiness. So were all the desires of our natures. Yet they are sources of pleasur only by their proper use. And we dayly see those who by an injudicious choice of the article they drink have destroyed their usefulness & the happiness of themselves and friends. Nothing produces a more lasting

66. Drew's earnings would have been "trusteed," i.e., garnished, if he had deserted his wife or otherwise failed to provide for the support of his wife and daughter.

67. Benjamin H. Piper worked for (or may have been a partner of) Peter S. Brown, a spoke manufacturer, and lived at 34 Bridge Street, according to the 1860 Manchester *Directory*.

& hopeless misery than a union with an unsuitable companion especially if he is intemperate (and in Drews case marriage cant take place). In such cases there is not hope but in *Death* and that may be looked & prayed for long in vain.

I am thankful you gave me information of the affair and doubt not that henseforth you will shun him as a serpent & such he realy is. Your Character, Health & Happiness presen[t] & future depend on your so doing.

You have now a good charracter (unless this has injured it). You have good looks & good health and if you prove yourself worthy may expect a good *Husband*.

Remember what I have told you about Mr. Drew is all true and is but a tythe[68] of what might be said of the same kind. Whilst I have recollection & reason I shal feel a deep interest in your prosperity & happiness and you will find in me & your mother friends at all *times*.

You spoke of attending a singing school. That is all very well if you can do so with propriety. But you had better spoil your voice & break your neck than go there or anywhere else to be attended by Mr. Drew. Your only safety is in renouncing him at *once* and *forever*.

And now good bye may the God of your & my Fathers keep you from all evil & make you wise & rich in time for eternity.

Luther M. Trussell

Delia M Page

New London Sept. 7, 1860

Dear Delia,

I should thank you for your very good letter. I am glad to know your health is good. I trust I shall ever feel a deep interest in your welfare.

You say you are not so much in love as we imagine; if so I am very glad of it. Not that I should not be willing you should love a worthy object but the one refered to is no doubt an *unworthy* one; and should you fix you affections on him, it will cause you sorrow such as you never knew; indeed we believe it would be *your ruin*. We have no reason to think, his pretensions notwithstanding, that he has any *real love for you*. Your father Trussell has told or rather written you what he has learned about him. I fear it will be hard for you to believe it, but if you will take the trouble to inquire, I think you will find it all true. He

---

68. Read as tithe, or tenth.

probably is incapable of even friendship, and in his apparent regard for you, is actuated by *low, base, selfish* motives.

I think you will sooner or later come to this conclusion respecting him. The sooner the better. Your reputation your happines all you hold dear are I fear at stake. You have done well, let not your high hopes be blasted. Do the best you can, keep no company but good and you stand fair to get a good husband, one who has a real regard for you. But if you keep this man's company, the virtuous must shun you. You will not like to read this. My only excuse for writing is that I am very anxious about you. If my anxiety is unfounded so much the better. Unfounded it cannot be if you are keeping the company of an unprincipled libertine.

Your affectionate Mother Trussell

[Sept. 7 1860]

My Dear Delia,

I am going to trouble you a little longer (I speak for the whole family now). In your situation you must necessarily form many new acquaintance[s] and amongst them there will be not a few who will assure you of their friendship and seek your confidence. The less worthy they are the more earnestly they will seek to convince you of their sincerity. You spoke of one girl whom you highly prised. I hope she is all that you think her to be. If so you are certainly fortunate in making her acquaintance.

But the best have failings & I should hardly expect one of her age a safe counciler in all cases. You must in fact rely upon a principal of morality within your own bosom and if you [are] at a loss you may depend upon the council of Mrs. Piper. A safe way is not to allow yourself to say or do anything that you would not be willing anyone should know if necessary. You will say Humpf think I cant take care of myself. I have seen many who thought so and found their mistake when ruined. My dear girl. We fear much for those we love much, or the fear is in porportion to the Love. And though I have no reason to think that you go out nights or engage in anything that will injure your health or morrals yet the love I have for you leads me to fear lest among so much that is plesant but evil you may be injured before you are aware of danger.

And now my Dear Girl I will finish by telling you what you must do for me.

You must take care of my little factory girl. Dont let her expose her health if you do she will be sick and loose [*sic*] all she has earned. Dont let her do any thing any time that she would be ashamed to have her father know. If you do she may loose her charracter. Try to have her improve some every day that she may be the wealthiest most respected & best beloved of all her sisters, brothers & kindred & so be fitted to make the best of husbands the best of wives.

[Luther M Trussell]

New London Sept. 11/60

My Dear Girl,

Your letter was received by Mondays mail. I am glad to hear you hold your weight so well. I think you have not pined much either with or for want of *Love*. Now I want you to screw your patience to a sticking point & moderate your love to summer temperature and read carefully that you may get my meaning. You know that I am willing you should marry as soon as the proper man is found. The onely difference between us is respecting the fitness of the individual.

You think I am mistaken in the charracter of Mr. Drew. I will tell you how I made up my mind (independent of the intelligence received from Man[che]ster). You told me he was about 28 yrs old, had obtained a divorce one child &c. Well I thought he was not very particular about the charracter of the lady he married or he would not have got into trouble so soon. Though if *he* had got the bill it was evident the court concidered her to blame, as he could not get a bill from her for his own misconduct. (But if she has a bill from him then he is the one in the fault.) Another thing is his paying attention to another lady whilst still bound to his wife. No person ought to do this & no one will who has a proper regard for the marriage institution and female charracter. The information received from M[anchester] confirmed my first impressions & I have seen nothing since to alter them. There must be a mistake if she had obtained a bill. He would not be liable for her debts unless previously contracted. And I do not see what need there is or how there can be a more complete separation. But he did not tell you at first that *he* had a bill of divorce or something to that effect. And has he not since said he was going to get one? Certainly I so read your letters and both cant be *true*. As I have no farther information respecting him I shall add nothing concerning his charracter. But [I] should be glad to say something that would benefit you if I could.

It cant be more unplesant for you to read this than it is for me to write. But my love for you & my duty require me to do it.

I do not ask you not to love him nor any one else. But I desire you to take the course I shall indicate as the one & onely one that will be safe for you whether he loves you or only *desires* you.

Make enquiries of those able to give you correct information. If he has told you the truth this will coroborate it. If he has told you false this will shew you what the truth is.

Treat him in company as you do other *Gentlemen* of your acquaintance and do not keep his company privately. Anything of this kind will be either known or suspected and might prevent his getting a bill if he is trying to obtain one. Permit no familiarities. They will only lower you in his estimation. For however unprincipaled a man may be, he always wishes for a virtuous wife. And one whose principals are strong enough for him to trust. When he is at liberty to give you his hand with his heart will be soon enough for intimacy. I wish you to understand distinctly that I wish you to keep entirely free from him however good he may be (and if he is good he will love you the more for it) untill he is in a condition to marry. Then if he is as worthy as you suppose I shall put no obstructions in the way.

You see I am but imperfectly acquainted with the business. I have not read as he has made the least advance to you. I have infered it from your letters. From all that you have yet written the *Love* may still be all on your side & it would not be the first case of the kind if it is. Look this over twice before you write & see if you cannot in your next give me all the information I need. And now my Dear Girl good bye. I know you are in great danger, but hope that God will preserve you from the snares of man and the temptations of the Devil.

L. M. Trussell.

D M Page

Manchester September the 20 1860

Mr. Trussell
Dear Sir,

I have been getting all the information concerning Delia that I could and will give it to you as you requested we should. In the first place there was a girl that boarded with Delia before she changed, that I was well acquainted with for she boarded with us a year. She is a pious good girl and Delia liked her very much. I thought I would go and see her. I asked her why Delia left. She said it was because Mrs. Crosby would not permit Drew to come there.[69] She liked Delia and told her she did not want her to leave but she could not have so base a man calling at her house and she chose to leave. Miss Perkins tried to get a chance to talk with her but she evaded her finally she got a chance to talk with her. Delia told her if she got into trouble no one would be to blame but herself. I thought I would not seek her but watch her movements. She does not come here much anyway. Yesterday when going down to Sarah Pittys funerel she told me she was comeing up to see me in the evening but she came up in the afternoon. In the course of conversation I asked her why she changed her boarding place. She said because she wanted to. She seemed to want to evade my enquiries. I thought I would not say eny thing to her about it if she did not to me but when she got ready to go I felt that I should be veryly guilty not to talk with her and I did. I told her the report was in this place that she was going with a man. She said she was. I told her he was a bad man. She said she did not think so and wanted to know who told me. I told her it come from a person who knew him well. I asked her what kind of a story he told her. She said he told her that he had never waited upon eny woman since he left his wife and some other things. I asked if she believed him [and] she said she did. I told her she did not know the treacherous and black heartedness of a villians heart and that of course he would keep a smooth tounge[sic] to her. I asked her if she had committed herself to him and she said she did not know as she had but it come out very faint. But I believe she intends to have him. She says she loves him.

Sept. 21

Since I commenced I have received more information. A girl that works in the room with Drew says that Delia is verry fond of him. She goes into his room to see him and then he goes into her room. She is conducting very improperly and it is creating a good deal of talk. The lady that she boarded with when she first came here has talked with her and it does no good. Mrs. Davis talked with her and asked her what Father Trussell would say if he knew it. She said he wouldent say much and then went on to say it was nothing to him. She was of age.

I do fear that she will be a ruind girl. I think all he wants is to get her money and then serve her as he has his wife. I have no doubt but he knows she has some for she loves him so well she would tell him I

69. Mrs. Crosby was Laura Crosby, keeper of the boardinghouse, 113 Amoskeag Company, where Delia resided. According to the city directory, Sylvester Drew lived nearby at 117 Amoskeag.

fear. (Some think she cares more about him then he does for her.)
Now what can we do to save her I know not. I have wrote the sum and
substance of what I gathered up until this time and will close.

yours respectfully

R. M. Piper[70]

━━━━━━━

New London Sept 25/60

My Dear Girl,

You were doubtless disappointed at not getting a letter on Saturday.
We could not get it mailed soon enough to go through. Mary has told
you I suppose all about our excertion to the mountain. A very pleasant
affair. I wish you could have gone with us.

We have a fine lot of apples a good crop of corn & potatoes & 95
bush[els] of wheat. So you can see we are in hoopes to have enough to
eat (though you know we dont have to eat onely half of it).

James Story & wife, George, Annette & Cate came up Friday eve.[71]
With the addition of G. Knowlton & Dickerson who board here and
the callers to see the boarders and visitors we have a large family and
pretty merry one too.

I suppose you are enjoying yourself as well as you *can*. Although the
circumstances that surround you are not the most desirable but as you
could not expect anything else I suppose you *Grin* and *bear* it (I am
very sorry that you attract so much notice just now). And as the season
is sickly I think it would be for your health & happiness to take a short
vacation. Visit us and your friends at NP[Newport] if you wish (they
say I wont let you visit them) and get rested for the work of a long
cold winter. We shall be glad to have you help us eat some very good
apples that we have. Get leave of absence as soon as you can for a few
weeks or as long as you choose & in your next let me know when you
can come and how long you can stay. Good by until next time and
hoping to both hear from you and see you too soon I will close.

Luther M. Trussell

Delia M Page

━━━━━━━

70. This letter is written by Rosaline Piper, Benjamin's wife and a native of
New London. 1850 Census of Manchester, dwelling 981; Lord, *History of New
London*, p. 251.
71. The reference is to Eliza Trussell's brother and his family, residents of
Hopkinton. Their daughter, Kate, lived in New London off and on in this
period and attended the Academy.

New London Novmr 16th 1860[72]

My Dear Girl,

I suppose you will be disappointed if you do not get a letter so I shal fold up a letter filled with ink marks & if you cannot decipher them it will make but little difference as I have nothing worth writing. We received your kind letter and are glad to see you have got over the dreaded trouble with so little dificulty.[73] The few real evils of life which must be met do not cause us half so much annoyance as the thousand immagined ones that we are constantly dreading but which like ghosts disappear on a near approach. The best (indeed the only right) way is to strictly adhere to principals of right. Under all circumstances to try in the first place to know what duty is and having determined this point perform it with out referance to what may be said about it. We are all able to make mistakes and it is a blessed priviledge that we can go to the fountain of Knowledge for that wisdom necessary to make the just decision.

Life to you seems long & old age so far off as neither to be dreaded or provided for. Yet a few years will place you as far along lifes road as Aunt Hitty & Uncle Amos now are & they can easily see to the natural end of their journey without glasses.

Try to live at all times & in all things so that in after years you may not have remorse instead of repentance. Spend your time wisely now and you need not dread wrincles white hairs or old age.

E[liza] and I went to Wilmot last Wednesday to a surprise party at the ministers.[74] It was a complete surprise so far as they were concerned. Between one & two hundred attended, rather a plesant affair on the whole. Aunt Sally Brown has just come in. And we expect Aunt Heath at Thanksgiving. I wish you could be here but no dout you will enjoy yourself better where you are. We are all in the usual health & hope to hear from you often.

L. M. Trussell

72. Seven weeks have passed since Luther Trussell's last letter to Delia, suggesting that Delia probably took a vacation in New London as her foster father advised.

73. Here we have the first indication that Delia may have cooled toward Drew.

74. Wilmot was the home of Luther's older brother, Ezekiel, whose son, Charles F. Trussell, was pastor of the Freewill Baptist Church. This party was probably held in honor of Charles. Lord, *History of New London*, p. 394.

New London Nov. 25 [1860]

My dear Delia,

You were no doubt disappointed in not receiveing a letter from us last night. We really ment to have written but various cercumstances combined to prevent. I had the headache a good part of the time last week and then L. had to take his turn, beside Aunt Heath is here and very ill.[75] Last night I feared she would have a feaver in spite of all I could do but she is better today. She says in her peculiar way, no one can be sick where I am, and that she has not had so much done for her this three years. I do hope she will be comfortable soon.

How glad I am that you have triumphed over your feelings. I know it must have cost you a hard struggle; but I trust you will ever rejoice in view of it and your friends too will rejoice with you, and all wether friends or not will respect you for the decided stand you have taken. Go on and may the blessing of the Most High attend your every effort to do right.

Thanksgiving is at hand, and we shall think of you; and if you could step in and spend the day with us we should like it. However I do no doubt you will have a good time. George expects to go home to his mother, intends getting the family all together.

It is very cold today so we are all staying at home except George who had a singing school at Sunapee last night, and has not returned.[76] I hope you will attend meting constantly, at least half a day every Sabbath. Your present and future welfare, I think, depend very much upon it.

Write often, at least once a fortnight, once a week when convenient, as we shall always feel an interest in your welfare.

Your foster mother,

Eliza S. Trussell

P.S. The next Wednesday after you left we had a good visit from the Rev. Mr. Arms and wife also Mr. and Mrs. Jones of Wilmot, and run [?] each other. They said they arranged to have come the week before.

Mr and Mrs Eastmond were here last week. They have not forgotten you. They seem the same as ever. We should have been glad if they could have come when you were here, as I think they would have had a better visit.

E.S.T.

---

75. Aunt Heath is Sally Trussell Heath, older sister of Luther. Lord, *History of New London*, pp. 166, 256.
76. Sunapee is the town just west of New London.

New London Dec. 19th 60

Dear Sister Delia,

We received your letter which was so long comeing yesterday. We looked and looked for a letter last week but looked in vane. We dident think it hardly fair of you when you had so much leasure time last week not to write. You must not do so again, you wont will you?

We have gone into the room you youst to have when you lived at home, to live on acount of Sarahs eyes. She likes the change much, so we all do. We killed our hog Monday (he wayed over 400 lb) & the cow. Come home now & you shant starve for as Aunt Heath sade we have got fresh meet, apples & potatoes enough. Your kitty Gray is well, we gave him away about a fortnight ago but he has not gone to his new home yet & I guess never will. Mr. Fowler where he was going isent very fond of cats.

Father is going to carry our letter to the P.O. so I can only add that Mother sends her love and says she would write if she hadent so much to do. Sarah cant write for fear of hurting her eyes. She too sends her love. I want to write ever so much but I suppose I cant.

There is one bit of news I must tell you. Mrs. Maria Farewell French has got a little baby about 2 weeks old. She has been 3 months married, we think her quite smart, dont you? Sarah has had sent her by the "Cosmopolitan art association" a large steel engraving (30 × 37) "Falstaff mustering his recruits." It is nice but I must not stop to write more. So good bye. Write soon to your

Affectionate Sister

Mary

New London Decm. 21/60

My ever Dear Girl,

I am going to write a few lines just to let you know that I can write yet though I guess you will find it hard to read.

You say you cannot make much just now. Stop & think. You make more than any man gets this season of the year who works on a farm. Keep up good courage if you cannot earn as much as you formerly have. Why, spend less and you will clear the same amount.

You are certainly fortunately situated and doing as well as anyone can expect to these times when there is little thought of but Niggers and little talked of but secession. Write soon and write just what comes into your head. No danger but it will be exceptable [sic] to us. I cannot write more now except, Dont be discouraged let what will come. You are a good girl. You will be a good woman, a good wife & I hope will have a good husband.

Luther M Trussell

New London Jany 15th 1861

My Dear Girl,

We received a welcome letter from you last week & were glad to know you were so comfortable these hard times. It appears you work on short time most mills are running in the same way.[77] Tell us how many days you can work a week. Dont neglect to keep an account of your expenses & make them as little as is consistent with health and decency. *Now* is *your time* to lay up for the *time* of *need*.

You mentioned Sylvester in your last. How is his divorce bill progressing? You say you have heard ever so many times that his wife is married. Well now I think few things would be easier than for Mr. Drew to assertain beyond a doubt whether she is married or not. And if he wished to know I think he would. I am not free from suspicions that he has not done anything about a divorce and if he has not the inferance is that he knows he would not succeed if he tries. This is suspicious & there may be not truth in it yet for anything I know to the conterary it may be all true.

I know no evil of Mr. Drew but at present I can but view him in an unfavourable light. A better acquaintance would remove my suspicions or confirm my fears.

I must again direct you to treat him as an acquaintance and nothing more untill such time as you have certain evidence that a more intimate relation will be neither criminal or disreputable. If he is a good man you will find it out before it is too late and if a bad one you cannot know it too soon.

I know something near what you will think if you dont speak it. That Father is scared to death of nothing. These are all lies that are told about Sylvester. Think I dont know? Well my Dear I think you *dont* know much more about it than I do and are far less qualefied to form an impartial opinion. I have nothing to bias my mind. My only desire in the case is your happiness. If Mr. Drew is the man who will most contribute to it I wish you to marry him. But first I wish for

---

77. Given mounting sectional tensions and the resulting shortage of cotton, New England textile mills reduced operations by cutting back the number of days they ran each week, hence the expression, "short time." Shorter hours, of course, meant a corresponding reduction in earnings.

reasonable evidence that he is sutch a man & next that he is legally free to do it. Whilst [things] remain as they are they now are (that is he legally debarred from intering into the matrimonial bonds) it is little less than madness for any body to treat him with more than cool politeness. Untill you have positive evidence that he is a free man you must treat him just as you would any respectable gentleman of your acquaintance.

Your onely safety lies in your adhering to the resolution with which you returned to the mills.[78] Adhere to this and all is well—abandon it and you are at once beyond my controll & you will very soon loose the controll of yourself. Good bye. But remember what I have written. Which is dictated by a pure desire that you might act wisely & prudently & not have cause of repentance when it is *too late*.

Luther M. Trussell

D M Page

New London Feb. 1/61

My Dear Girl,

Your last letter was received the day it was mailed. And if you were a little crusty when you wrote I laughed heartily when I read thinking what a figure you would present taking vengence on your adversaries. I believe you had better let them run untill they are fatter. Now be patient and I will tell you all I can about it. Who started the story I dont know. How extensively it was circulated I dont know. Whether anyone believed it or not I dont know. But as you say it is false I feel as though I know that it was not so. I can believe you.

But you need not blame anyone in particular. No one has given me any information on the subject except at my request. My duty requires me to asertain the facts if I can. I have inquired of such onely as I thought could give me correct information.

Mr. and Mrs. Haines will be here this evening. I shal enquire of them and any other persons I may hereafter see who I suppose able to throw light on the subject.

I do not ask them if you are going to be married or if Mr. Drew is married, but if they are acquainted with a man by the name of Drew what of him.

I am glad to hear of your resolution to increase your deposit to

78. These lines support the earlier suggestion that Delia had returned to New London in October and November, and that her stay had played an important role in her break with Drew.

[$]100, but I do not wish you to kill yourself to do it. Nor shal I blame you if you get the silk dress first, but be that as you please.

We shal send you a few things & would send more if they could be taken care of. But [maple] sugar time is not far off when I expect you will eat bacon & apples with us. Untill then have patience and courage. Keep your eyes & ears open. See & hear for yourself. All may yet turn out for the best. That it may is the sincere prayer of a disinterested friend.

Luther M. Trussell

D M Page

New London Sunday March 1861

Dear Delia,

It is Sunday agen but I shall not go to church today, for Mr. French and his wife are gone to Henniker[79] with the horse and it blows so hard I *cant* walk; George and mother have tryed to make me go but if they hated to walk in the wind as bad as I do with their clows [clothes] blowd up to their knees I guess they would stay at home. I wouldent be hired to go up there a foot to day. Mother is not going she isent able to.

Next Wednesday I have got to speak a piece. I am in Miss Ambrose class in composition. I am going to speak a piece called "The Dreamer and the Worker". It is excerlent. The first verse is:

"See the dreamer in his life boat"
Idle oars are at his side,
And his boat is rising, falling,
On the deep and silent tide.

There is 12 verses fore lines in each.

I have a room with Martha, Mary and Hellen Andrews at the Boarding house. It is the back attic, this end, Mary and Hellen are all the time or most all the time talking about the gentlemen. Oh! dear I have got sick of the idea; such a one M. says is pretty. H says "yes if he want so dreadfull green." But a few days ago they were all taken up with a gentleman that goes to school (he is pretty and he knows every body thinks so) and talked about him half the time. Yesterday when he was going up to the Hall they saw him and Hellen sade she thought "he was auwfle homely." Mary asked her how long she had thought

---

79. Henniker is in the southern part of Merrimack County, about twenty-two miles south of New London.

so. She sade ever since he came down to their house (the boys come down there a bit). They sade he looked kinder pretty with his red shirt on but without it he was so homely! For my part I think he looks as well as they do, but I must'ent talk about my neighbors any more. You must forget every word I have sade.

George has gon to meeting and dident know but Dyar would come home with him. He ment to have him. He is going to bring his melodian up as soon as he can have Mr. Frenchs horse to do it with.

Do you and Sammantha get along well together? And how does Mr. Sylvester Drew do? How are Mr. Haynes folks?[80] You go with wagons down there by this time, dont you? Our snow is leaveing us fast. Poor William has had to keep house all alone for three days. Dont you "spose" he thinks of Ellen and the sider mill some times? They had an exerbition at Sutton last week and Will went and Ellen went and Mr. Andrew[s] sade he never saw a softer looking couple in his life, proably not since his courting days!

Susan Craft has one beau left yet. Crage, he went to school a year ago last fall. He has come up to Mr. Crafts *and it must be* to see Susan. He went to meeting with her last Sunday and sat with her all day and went home with her at night afoot. Though John went up after her with a horse but they had got the start of him.[81]

Now my letter is long enough but there isent much in it but I wont write any more. I wont, I wont, I vow I wont. Perhaps you wont think that very pretty language but Miss Mary and Miss Hellen Andrews say that a great deal and "you confounded fool" is a great word with them.

Well my dear Dill you wont get out of patience at my ribble rabble will you? I wont write any more till I have something more of consequence to write. Good bye.

Yours truly Minnie [Mary]

P.S. "Ive thought one something sur." George Sanders has bought a little house and a quarter of an acker for his father and mother. Aint he a good boy? that indeed. Mr. Culver from Hopkinton I think is here taking ambrotypes. A great many have had theirs taken. I should like to have mine but I had it taken so many times last summer that we

---

80. Mrs. Haynes was a New London native, Caroline Knowlton Haynes, who lived in Manchester. A cousin of Luther Trussell, she carried letters and packages between Delia and her foster family. Lord, *History of New London,* pp. 118, 260-61; Manchester *Directory,* 1858, 1860.

81. "Crage's" interest appears to have been reciprocated; Susan Craft and Isaac Craig were married Nov. 24, 1864. Lord, *History of New London,* p. 339.

cant afford it. Please excuse the first I wrote and forget the last. After you have read this burn it up and I will thank you 4000 times.

Good bye once more

Yours Minnie

Today is town meeting day and George has been writeing votes as fast as his pen could travel.

Manchester N.H. April 14/61

My Dear Little Sister,[82]

How do you do this afternoon? What are you doing, reading some good story I presume, or helping mother washing the dishes perhaps? How I do wish I could step in and see you a little while. What a good time we would have wouldn't we? I wish you could come and see me in my little attic, if I stay all summer you must come here. I will meet you at the Depot any time. I am not sure of working all summer if they only work on short time I think I shall stay here. I wish they would work until the first of July as they have done and then stop a few weeks. Then I would come home but nobody knows what they will do.

What did you do fast day?[83] I went up to Mr. Haynes' in the forenoon and took dinner. In the afternoon I had my picture taken and in the evening I went to my cousins in Squag.[84] I enjoyed myself very well. How are Sarah's eyes now? I do pity her so. I wish I could see her. Tell her if there is any little thing that she wants to write and tell me what it is and when I come home I will bring it to her. Tell her to keep up good courage. I hope her eyes will be better when it comes warm weather. Tell mother I wish she would have her miniature taken and sent to me. I want to get a frame. I suppose it would be useless to ask for Sarah's but I should like it very much. Oh, Mary, if I could only write what I think of while I am to work you would have a nice long letter but when I sit down to write I cant think of a thing. I have got so far and I cant get any farther. You hav'nt written to me for a

82. This letter is addressed to Delia's foster sister, Mary Trussell.
83. Fast Day was a traditional New Hampshire holiday dating from the seventeenth century when provincial residents had fasted and prayed for the recovery of an ill Lieutenant Governor. He died, but the holiday, generally celebrated in April, continued.
84. Read as "Squog," short for Picatasquog, the river which joins the Merrimack just south of Manchester.

Manchester N.H. April 14 /61.

My Dear Little Sister:

How do you do this afternoon? What are you doing reading some good story I presume; or helping mother. washing the dishes perhaps. How I do wish I could step in and see you a little while. What a good time we would have wouldn't we? I wish you could come and see me in my little attic. if I stay all summer you must come here. I will meet you at the Depot any time. I am not sure of working all summer if they only work on short time I

Delia Page letter, 1861.

great while. You must write as soon as you get this and write a good long letter. I want you all to write this time. Give my love to all. Goodbye.

Your Sister,

Delia

M. K. Trussell
New London, N.H.

Two women weavers, c. 1860.

Afterword

THE CONCLUSION of the mill correspondence of Delia Page and her foster family brings us to the end of an era. With the coming of the Civil War and the ensuing short supply of raw cotton, a large number of textile manufacturing firms in New England closed their doors. Other mills, like those of the Amoskeag Company in Manchester, went on short time, running only a few days each week in an effort to stretch out limited supplies. In either event, the war period marked a severe discontinuity in mill employment. Yankee farm daughters began to look elsewhere for opportunities and, when regular production resumed at the end of the fighting, the mills came increasingly to be staffed by immigrant operatives or their children. The Irish dominated the work force initially, but over time increasing numbers of French Canadians entered the mills as well.

Thus, the letters contained in this volume delineate the mill experience of Yankee women in a distinct and limited era, the antebellum decades. It might be useful at this point to discuss briefly the broad picture presented by the letter writers and consider as well what mill women did *not* write about.

Two factors contribute to a sense of timelessness in the letters. First, there is very little in a given collection that places it at a fixed moment in time. Mary Paul does describe the 1848 electioneering of the Whigs and Free Soilers and Mary Trussell is enthusiastic about the Republican candidates in the 1860 election but, except for these occasional references, there is little in the letters that would permit us to place them in a chronological sequence. Second, there is a basic homogeneity about the lives of Yankee mill women as revealed in the letters. With the exception of the Sanborn family in Nashua in the mid-1840s, all of the women lived in boardinghouses while working in the mills. They left their families and worked for a limited number of years before marriage. Economic motivations loomed large in the women's decisions to enter the mills and most of the letter writers note their wages or savings at some point in their correspondence. Finally, whether the date is 1830 or 1860, we see evidence in the letters of a newfound social and cultural independence among the women who left their farming homes to live and work in the growing mill towns.

In view of this timeless quality in the letters, two things are strikingly absent. First, in reading them one has no sense of the broader economic and political conflicts that arose in the mills of this period. There are no references to the strikes in Lowell and other mill towns in the mid-1830s or to the petition campaigns of the Ten Hour Movement of the 1840s when thousands of women called upon State Legislatures to shorten the hours of labor within the mills. Furthermore, we get a very limited sense of the dramatic transformation of the mill towns and mill employment over this thirty-year period. From the letters alone we may derive a sense of the everyday lives of women, but not of the dramatic confrontations of the period nor of the broad changes that distinguished mill life in 1860 from that thirty years earlier.

Newspaper accounts, protest petitions and broadsides, and the letters of mill agents are our chief sources for reconstructing the labor protests of women in the mill towns of the 1830s and 1840s. In my research I have found only two contemporary, unpublished references to mill protest written by workers. In February 1834, an operative, Mary Hall, recorded several diary entries during the first strike in Lowell's history. She noted on February 14: "To day some excitement amongst the girls of the Factories respecting the wages and many of the girls have left work." The next day she wrote: "The excitement increases & many more have left."[1] Mary Hall does not appear to have been among those leaving work and the sense of distance communicated in these lines suggests that she was something of a bystander on the fringes of the protest. A decade later, Daniel Spencer Gilman, a Canadian working in Lowell, offered a more sympathetic view of labor protest. Gilman joined the local Mechanics and Laborers' Association and wrote for its newspaper, *The Operative*. He represented Lowell workers at a Boston convention of the New England Workingmen's Association, and his letters offer a view of local activities on behalf of the Ten Hour Movement. In particular, he demonstrates the crucial role played by working women in this campaign.[2]

1. Mary Hall Diary, Feb. 14 and 15, 1834, New Hampshire Historical Society.
2. Daniel Spencer Gilman Letters, Brome County Historical Society, Knowlton, Quebec. Several of the letters are to be reprinted in Thomas Dublin, "A Personal Perspective on the Ten Hour Movement," forthcoming in *Labor History*.

Among letter writers in this volume, Mary Paul provides at least brief glimpses of some of these aspects of mill life. Comments in one of her letters suggest she suffered under the speedup system, although she does not refer to it by name. She complains, in her letter of November 5, 1848: "I never worked so hard in my life." This was a period in which mill management sought to step up the pace of work and reduce unit labor costs, and Mary may well have been feeling the pressure resulting from these efforts. In addition, she records the wage cut imposed in the Lowell mills in November 1848 and notes that it caused "a good deal of excitement" in anticipation. Unfortunately the next surviving letter in the collection is dated July 1849, fully seven months after the wage cut, and she does not offer a view of the reaction itself.

Other letter writers appear to have been working during periods of labor protest, but correspondence has not survived from these years. The Sawyer sisters began working in Lowell in 1835, but whether or not they participated in the strike of October 1836 is not clear. They were not as distant from the protests as the focus of their letters might suggest. We know that Louisa Sawyer took part in the Ten Hour Movement, for she signed an 1846 petition calling for a reduction of the hours of labor in the mills.[3] This fact suggests that we cannot infer women's attitudes or actions from the silences in their letters. We should be wary of dividing mill women into activists, on the one hand, and more articulate letter writers, on the other. The public writings of the protestors suggest they were "literary" in their own right, and the women's letters give indications of values that are certainly consistent with those expressed in the protests. Mary Paul, for instance, was skeptical of the justifications the mill agents gave for their impending wage reduction in November 1848. In a subsequent letter, she noted with evident approval that men and women were paid the same wages for their work at the North American Phalanx. While there is no direct evidence that Mary Paul joined the Female Labor Reform Association or worked for the ten-hour day, there are numerous indications in her letters that she might have been responsive to the appeals made by the movement's leaders.

Also strikingly absent from the letters of mill women is any reference to immigrants. In the years between 1830 and 1860 the proportion of immigrants in the mills rose sharply. At the Hamilton Company in Lowell, the foreign-born comprised less than 4 percent in 1836. By 1845 this proportion had risen slowly to 8 percent, but thereafter the number of immigrants working in the mills shot up. By 1860, immigrants comprised

3. Petition 11983 (1846), Massachusetts State Archives.

more than 61 percent of the Hamilton work force. For the Pemberton Mill in neighboring Lawrence, an even greater 78 percent were foreign born.[4]

We can account for the absence of references to immigrants in mill letters in a number of ways. First, a fair share of the correspondence antedates the entrance of large numbers of immigrants into the mills. There were few Irish in the mills when Sarah Hodgdon, Wealthy Page, and Persis and Malenda Edwards worked in Lowell, Great Falls, and Nashua. Even those Yankee women who entered the mills in the late 1840s and 1850s, however, were somewhat sheltered from interactions with the Irish. If the Hamilton Company in Lowell is at all typical, it appears that mill management made a consistent effort to segregate immigrant and native-born within both the mills and the boardinghouses. Immigrant workers were confined, initially at least, to the low-paying carding and spinning rooms, leaving the more skilled jobs in the dressing and weaving rooms to Yankee workers. Furthermore, immigrants resided in subsidized company housing in much smaller numbers than one would expect. At the Hamilton Company, in 1850, immigrant women made up 40 percent of the work force but comprised only 8 percent of female residents in the company boardinghouses. One New Hampshire firm bought a boardinghouse on the outskirts of town to provide housing for immigrants while keeping them at a distance from Yankee workers.[5] Thus, even though there were Irish in the mills when Louisa Sawyer and Delia Page were working, it is unlikely that they had much direct contact with the newcomers.

The omissions in these letters suggest how important it is to supplement the picture one derives from women's correspondence with evidence drawn from other sources. Contemporary newspapers, protest petitions and broadsides, and company records and correspondence all serve to broaden our view of women's lives in the antebellum textile mills. To date, very few private letters, diaries, or reminiscences of immigrants have surfaced, but it will only be a matter of time and digging before we have primary materials from their perspective as well.[6]

The letters presented in this volume offer a rich source for understand-

4. Thomas Dublin, *Women at Work*, pp. 26, 139; Clarisse Poirier, "Pemberton Mills, 1852-1938: A Case Study of the Industrial and Labor History of Lawrence, Massachusetts," (Ph.D. diss., Boston University, 1978), p. 125.

5. Dublin, *Women at Work*, pp. 139, 155-56.

6. Brian Mitchell, "Immigrants in Utopia: The Early Irish Community of Lowell, Massachusetts, 1821-1861" (Ph.D. diss., University of Rochester, 1980), has unearthed a number of important new sources on Lowell's Irish Catholic Church, although private letters have not been among them.

ing the human dimensions of early industrialization in this country. Women mill workers, however, are probably the most thoroughly studied working-class group in these decades, and we must expand our vision to include shoe workers, tailors and seamstresses, domestic servants, urban artisans, and others. They all had to make their peace with the rise of industrial capitalism in these years, and they shaped the new institutions that arose as much as they were themselves molded in the process. The challenge to the social historian is to study both the broad contours of change and the individual responses to these developments and to delineate the social and psychological processes that link these two levels. As we begin to construct a picture of the larger setting in nineteenth-century America, we may better understand the place of Yankee mill women in the transformation that established industrial capitalism in this country.